What Reviewers Wrote About "A MATTER OF FAITH"

"He survived the Nigerian-Biafra war; but emotional scars remained, and he was simply living for the moment without regard to ultimate purpose, anxious to begin his new married life in the United States, studying computer science. He was on the fast track to success until the stock market crashed and layoffs forced him into dire circumstances in which he lost his life savings, his wife and kids, and everything he'd worked for. It should be noted that the process of redefining his faith-based life is nicely wound into the general autobiography. Many details are provided about his life and its progression. This focus on Ndukwe's course is a reminder that *A Matter of Faith* is about how the author reconnected with his overall purpose: of necessity, autobiographical depth is a part of exploring this journey. Readers who like autobiographical pieces that traverse personal, business, and religious growth alike will appreciate the focus of Ndukwe's story, about reconnecting with God in a different way."

—The Midwest Reviews

I am happy to rate this book 3 out of 4 stars. His testimony enriches my own faith, and I wholeheartedly recommend this book for men and women of all age groups. There is nothing graphic or disturbing enough for children not to read it, but it is suitable for teenagers and adults. Those involved in computer engineering and technology may benefit from the author's experiences.

—OnlineBookClub Reviews

He's laid off from multiple jobs as the companies continue to go under, and he's forced to move around the country in order to keep paying rent and keep pursuing his dreams. Readers have the pleasure of following a brilliant and kindhearted young man who doesn't give up in *A Matter of Faith*.

We open the memoir as Ndukwe is on a plane to the United States, only weeks away from starting the collegiate school year. Thanks to a little help from strangers and his own brilliant mind, Chuks excels in school and starts to impress every boss he comes in contact with. His excellence in engineering sends readers toward a place of success and positivity until the economic recession takes hold. While the twists and turns keep us guessing, perhaps the finest aspect of this book is the storyline of hope, resilience, and the faith that keeps the author afloat in his trying times. He encounters not only the issue of being laid off multiple times, but he has to traverse through a troublesome marriage and a scam that threatens to steal all of his hard-earned money. But despite these extreme hardships, he continues to keep fighting. I couldn't help but root for Chuks as a reader, clinging to the page and hoping that the good he shares with the world will come back around to him.

Overall, *A Matter of Faith* is an enjoyable read that many could benefit from reading. Chuks is a genuinely likeable person to follow around. If you're in the mood for an inspiring story of overcoming hardships and don't mind the editorial issues, this could prove to be a truly worthwhile read for you.

—Independent Book Review

We have resolved each reviewer's issues through final editing and made this book truly enjoyable.

Also by Chuks I. Ndukwe
Available everywhere

The Courage To Aspire

A MATTER OF FAITH

How Faith Saved Me From Homelessness

Chuks I. Ndukwe

A MATTER OF FAITH:
How Faith Saved Me From Homelessness.

Copyright © 2018 by Chuks I. Ndukwe
All Rights Reserved.

This publication may not be reproduced in whole or in part. It may not be transmitted in any form or means, electronic or mechanical, or stored in a retrieval system. There may be no mechanical copying, photocopying, recording, or otherwise, without express written permission by the publisher.

Publisher's Cataloging-In-Publication Data
(Prepared by The Donohue Group, Inc.)

Names: Ndukwe, Chuks I., 1942- author.
Title: A matter of faith: how faith saved me from homelessness / Chuks I. Ndukwe.
Description: [Newark, New Jersey] : Ikebiebooks, [2019] | Includes bibliographical references.
Identifiers: ISBN 9780999070574 (paperback) | ISBN 0999070576 (paperback) | ISBN 9780999070581 (ebook)
Subjects: LCSH: Ndukwe, Chuks I., 1942---Religion. | Faith. | Money--Religious aspects--Christianity. | Homelessness--Religious aspects--Christianity.
Classification: LCC BV4637 .N38 2019 (print) | LCC BV4637 (ebook) | DDC 234/.23--dc23

ISBN: 9780999070574   (Trade Paperback)
ISBN: 0999070776
ISBN: 9780999070581   (Ebook)

LCCN: 2018912517

For information regarding publisher's permission contact:
Ikebiebooks Publishing
info@ikebiebooks.com
855-336-7770

Dedication

To those who survived adversities without selling their soul.

Contents

Epigraph x
Prologue xi
Chapter 1 1
   Coming To America 1
Chapter 2 10
   Always On My Mind 10
Chapter 3 19
   The Essence of Work Study 19
Chapter 4 27
   Software Then Hardware 27
Chapter 5 46
   Welcome To High Tech 46
Chapter 6 54
   How Caller ID Began 54
Chapter 7 67
   Following The Guide 67
Chapter 8 77
   Problem Solver 77
Chapter 9 92
   Sad Ending 92
Chapter 10 114
   They Won't Let Go 114
Chapter 11 121
   Marriage And Children 121
Chapter 12 135
   Defrauded 135
Chapter 13 144

A MATTER OF FAITH

    Helping Hands 144
Chapter 14 149
    Faith And Courage 149
Chapter 15 149
    Keeping The Pledge 156
    Epilogue 169
    Acknowledgements 173
    About the Author 175
Other Books By Chuks I. Ndukwe 176

Epigraph
★★★

As we take the journey of life, the task is not to worry about the twists and turns and its direction nor dwell on how it will end. But to remain true to who we are and firm in our beliefs. For inside us is incredible interiority complex. [Irresistible inner-power, that guides the journey; conscience, the judge between right and wrong; non-carnal senses that see past the bright light of the day and the darkness of night to preview events that lie ahead, and the inner-voice that counsels us]. These four elements of life function in a contingent symbiosis to move the journey along the guardrails of a natural order. A day will come when our work on earth is compared with our reason for being. Ultimately, it is if and only if our work on earth matches our reason for being could we honestly say, "yes, this is my destiny."

Prologue

There are only two ways to live your life. One is as though nothing is a miracle. The other is as though everything is a miracle.

~ Albert Einstein

I had survived the Nigerian-Biafra war; tried my best to deal with the physical wounds. But the emotional scars? That seemed a little too much. Regardless, the will to live and hope for better tomorrow kept pushing us ahead—everybody—boys and girls, men and women, the young and the old. My dad had talked about the journey—the apt metaphor for life, but I did not think about it the same way. I did not know anybody who did. Instead, I was simply living in the moment—one day at a time while all the unknown—future milestones lay yet ahead. I was twenty-two at the time, six years out of technical college, a high school teacher, married four days before, and anxious to start a new life in the United States and study computer science.

I had not seen the airport before that moment when I arrived at the Lagos International Airport with my newlywed and Uncle Anyele Ochu. I recall watching planes descend to a landing and others ascend into the sky, and thought "Wow! I will be inside that flying object soon."

Suddenly, the helter-skelter movement of people around the terminal reminded me of the many chaotic moments when people moved, in the same way, to escape the bomb blast during the war.

The terminal was filled with passengers and people who came to see them off. After checking in my luggage, my wife and I walked around the terminal, checking the arrival and departure monitors. Then we sat at the boarding gate and chatted until the sound system announced my boarding, and then I hugged her at the departure gate and proceeded to board the plane.

Now seated inside the magnificent KLM 747, I remembered the effect of the war again—villages demolished, lives destroyed, families ripped apart, a nation in turmoil, and my dad. Then I sought comfort in the belief that I'd return soon to join his second wife and my older brother, Dick to take care of him. Suddenly, a gentleman took his seat beside me. We introduced ourselves; his name was Dr. Ekpo Ekong. He asked if I was traveling for the first time, and then he asked if anybody was waiting for me on my arrival in the United States. I was not sure, so I gave him my college admission letter. After reading the letter, he assured me that he would take care of me until I started school.

So, I lived with Dr. Ekpo Ekong and his wife, Andrea, until I started school at Honeywell Institute of Computer Science in Burlington, Massachusetts. Then the school arranged for me to live with Mrs. Terry Zdanauk.

One day, I learned from reading the Boston Globe that Northeastern University operated a co-operative system of education. "The system enriches students with both academic and technical expertise upon graduation." So, I transferred to Northeastern University to pursue studies in the combined computer science and electrical engineering in 1975.

As it turned out, my decision seemed excellent because I had attended a college with a similar system of education and enjoyed the benefits that the network offers. Here's how it works: students spend the full freshman and senior years in school without a summer break. Then they spend the intervening years alternating between the classroom and the industry on a co-op program—the "co-op" quarterly until their graduation day. I worked full time when I was not on co-op and went to school full time. Looking back, I must say "the co-op played an invaluable part of my college education. Because each successive period made me more intimately familiar with the bright and blurry spots of the high-tech industry.

A MATTER OF FAITH

Sure, graduating with a degree in electrical engineering was important. However, it was the advanced knowledge I acquired in computer and electrical engineering through the co-op that excited me.

So, after my graduation, I worked for Spectrametrics before returning to school to continue my studies in computer science. Then I worked for other companies such as USRobotics, ADC Telecommunications, and Lucent Technologies, managing a department that designed the internet gateways before the economy crashed in 2001.

I was at the top of my game when the stock market crashed. And took the economy along with it. As a result, Lucent laid off over forty thousand workers. However, the executive staff did not want to let me go, so they transferred me to Bell Labs—Lucent's research division. Finally, in 2001, the situation became dire, prompting the company to lay me off. Then I panicked; purchased a franchise, which was a scam, and lost my savings.

After searching for a job in the high tech industry for four straight years and unable to find one, I tried marketing only to discover how badly I sucked at it. And then I moved on to freelance messenger services for the sake of survival; that too did not work out well.

For whatever reason, everything that could go wrong did and I had nothing left but headache, hopelessness, and dismay. So I sought guidance in the words of the bible and mustered the courage to ask God for rescue. Now, as if I sat on Daddy's burnt-out-laps to asked him why he took away my toys, I asked God for a job and money. Then I decided to go out to a company I had passed many times without bothering to ask for a job and drop off my résumé.

Miraculously, as I stepped outside to check if I had enough gas in my car, I found a ten-dollar bill on the cover of a utility hole in the parking lot. Then I went to that company to drop off my résumé and got the job too.

I was a few hours away from knocking on the doors of the homeless shelter to ask for a bed, and I had asked God for rescue. So thinking about God's quick response, and where I am today, the title of this book "A Matter Of Faith" jumped right out at me.

Chapter 1
Coming To America

I may not have gone where I intended to go, but I think I have ended up where I needed to be.

~ Douglas Adams

On my last night in Nigeria—Lagos to be exact, December 9, 1972, The weather was hot and humid. Amidst tosses and turns and soaking sweat, my wife, Fortune and I managed occasional sleep here and there. The following day, the weather was a bit nicer so between reminiscing about the first time we met, our lives in Port Harcourt, and our experiences there as well as events before, during, and after the war, we grabbed naps to make up for the lost sleep. Talking as we were, I kept getting soft jabs; Evidently, I was not giving my full attention; my mind was partially on the notion of the journey as an apt metaphor for life.

Suddenly I got a hard push, and then I stopped thinking about the journey; its direction, or how it would end. I had already seen many horrific things in my short life that I did not dwell on nor worry about. "There must be a power in me that is guiding me," I thought silently.

"Why did you push me like that," I asked fortune.

"You seem to be dreaming or simply ignoring me," she replied.

"I am sorry," I apologized "my mind was on some shit my dad talks about frequently."

"What was that, not to marry a river girl?"

"No, something about life," I said and urged her to change the topic.

In the evening, Uncle Anyele Ochu and Fortune escorted me to the airport and then at eight o'clock, I boarded the plane. As I sat in the plane thinking about the world I was leaving behind—villages devastated by the war, lives destroyed, hopes shattered, families ripped apart, and the nation in turmoil, this tall, handsome black man carrying a garment bag walked to my seat, put his luggage in the overhead bin, and sat next to me.

The weather was mildly hot, the sky blue, while gentle breeze caressed those who walked around the serene-looking tarmac. Then after a short wait, the plane taxied majestically along the tarmac to the takeoff spot. "Ladies and gentlemen, the plane is ready for a takeoff. Fasten your seat belts," the pilot announced.

Shortly, the plane took off with a loud noise. The front end nosed upward and climbed into the sky. Through the window, I saw the entire city of Lagos as outlined by electric lights; it looked beautiful from the air, and then it diminished in size and went out of view.

Suddenly, another announcement came over the sound system: "Ladies and gentlemen, we are cruising at thirty-four-thousand feet altitude. The Fasten Seat Belt sign is off. You are free to walk around."

Now I am thinking—this gentleman sitting next to me looks like my brother so when I saw him, I liked him at that instant. Soon the cabin got very cold, so he asked for two blankets; he gave me one and covered himself with the other.

"My name is Ekpo Ekong," he said.

"My name is Ogbuleke Ikebie Ndukwe."

"Where are you traveling to?"

"Boston, United States."

"Which part of Boston?"

"Burlington."

"Are you going there to attend school?"

"Yes, I am sir."

"Which school?"

"It is the Honeywell Institute of Computer Science."

"Does the school know that you are coming today?"

"I am not sure, but they sent me this letter," I said and handed my admission letter to him.

"I am glad we met," he said. "You'll stay with me until you start school."

From that moment, he began to act like my older brother—he showed me the emergency equipment and the toilet in case I needed to

A MATTER OF FAITH

use it. Shortly, when the hostesses came around for service, he ordered two of everything; one for me and one for himself.

"I am a doctor in Boston, and my wife is a nursing manager, and we both work at Boston General Hospital," he said. "I came home to visit my family members who survived the war. How did you survive the war?"

"I was an electrical supervisor at the Nigerian Refinery at Eleme, Port Harcourt, before the war," I said, "so during the war, I built electrical systems for the Biafran Refineries, hence I was well protected, but I lost my mother and my brother."

"Where did you train to be that good in electrical engineering?"

"I attended UAC Technical College in Sapele."

"My cousin attended that college, and he is a manager at the port authority in Calabar," he said. "You could take over the management of the refinery if you stayed in Nigeria."

"That could have happened, but the federal government would not allow the Ibos back at the refineries after the war."

"Ladies and gentlemen fasten your seat belts," the pilot announced as the plane entered a state of turbulence.

Then after a few more hours, following the sunrise, the plane descended with less jerky movements and steadied again. It kept doing that until another announcement sounded: "Prepare for landing."

Meanwhile, the hostesses walked around, making sure everybody had his or her seat belt on, and the seats were in their upright positions. Then the plane dived, hit the ground with a little jolt, and taxied to the gate.

"Ladies and gentlemen welcome to Schiphol Airport, Amsterdam," the pilot announced, directing passengers to their connecting flights.

Shortly after the plane landed, Dr. Ekong and I walked to the terminal where the plane that would take us to JFK International Airport in New York was minutes away from taking off. As luck would have it, we barely crossed the boarding gate before the door slammed shut behind us. Then after a few more hours cruising in the sky, we arrived at JFK International Airport, where Dr. Ekong directed me to the immigration services to process my F1 visa. Then we took another plane to Logan Airport in Boston.

Upon our arrival at Logan, Mrs. Andrea Ekong was waiting for her husband.

"Welcome back. I missed you," Mrs. Ekong said.

"I missed you too," he replied. "This is Ogbuleke Ikebie Ndukwe. He is on his way to Honeywell Computer School in Burlington. We met on the plane, and he does not know anybody in the United States, so he will stay with us until he finds a place to live, if it is OK with you." Then he turned to me and said: "This is my wife, Andrea."

"I am glad to meet you," she said.

"I am glad to meet you too," I replied.

Outside the terminal, snow rained, covering my entire body. It was an awful—unwelcome combination of surprise and culture shock that made me want to turn around and go back if I could. Now sensing my discomfort, Mrs. Ekong let me in the car fast, put our luggage in the trunk, started the car, and a few minutes later, the car warmed me up.

"Take us to the mall," Dr. Ekong said.

When we got there, the parking lot was packed, but Mrs. Ekong found a space to park. Then we made our way inside the mall—a galactic arrangement of stores I could never have imagined displaying different merchandise. We weaved around the upper level, then the lower level to Burlington Coat Factory, where Mrs. Ekong picked out a coat, hats, gloves, and a pair of sweaters to go with it.

"These will last you through the winter," Mrs. Ekong said.

Getting back in the car, I slept all the way, till we arrived in Newton, Massachusetts, where Dr. and Mrs. Ekong lived. It was so cold in that colonial house that my sweater did not keep me warm. So under the spell of that freezing cold, I curled up in bed, covered myself with sheets and blankets, and dared anybody to drag me out for dinner. Sure as I expected, the maid tried but failed.

The following morning, the maid tried again, but I was still too cold to oblige. At this time, Dr. and Mrs. Ekong had gone to church, and the maid was about to enter the guest room to perform her morning chore. Now the moment of shame and ridicule was upon me—I had peed in the bed, and I could smell it; yes, it was I-can't-believe-I-did-

A MATTER OF FAITH

this moment. Somehow, I overcame my shame and told the maid when she came around again. "It's OK. I will give you another sheet," she said and collected the wet ones.

"Can you wash my clothes too?" I asked.

Then she collected my clothes, left the room, and came back with cleaning fluid and wiping cloth and wiped off the mattress.

"Don't lie on the bed until I put the sheets on the mattress," she said. "You should come out and eat breakfast."

Still shy from peeing in the bed, I sat down feeling embarrassed, ate breakfast, and watched TV until she made the bed up; then I lay back in bed. At lunch, I had warmed up enough, so I got out of the sheets and joined her for lunch.

On Monday, Dr. Ekong escorted me to Honeywell Institute of Computer Science in Burlington and spoke to the dean of admissions, and then he told me that Mrs. Ekong would pick me up on her way home from work. Shortly, the dean registered me for classes, which had started two weeks before. As Dr. Ekong had told me, Mrs. Ekong picked me up at three-thirty. And for the first week, I attended school from Dr. Ekong's house following the drop-off-pick-up routine.

When class ended on December 15, the dean informed me that he had arranged for me to live with Mrs. Terry Zdanauk at 11 College Road in Burlington and advised his secretary to give me a ride there. When we arrived at Terry's house at four o'clock in the afternoon, she brought her children and me together.

"Hey, guys, we have company," she said. "I can't pronounce his name."

But she introduced me to her children: Dan, Andy, Renee, and Billy.

"Where did you get that funny name?" Dan asked.

"Where are you from?" Andy asked.

"I am from Nigeria," I replied.

"He'll be attending Honeywell School down in the mall area," Terry said. "Just so you know, he will be living here with us, so be nice to him."

"How do you pronounce your name?" Renee asked.

As I tried to help them, they gave up before I did.

Because the school was further than a walking distance, Terry gave me a ride back and forth to school for one week. Usually, when I came home after school, the first thing I'd do was to try and get some sleep, but Billy would knock on my door, grab my hand and walk out to the living room. Then he'd bring out a bunch of noisy toys for us to play with. I can tell you I am not somebody who feels bothered by a kid wanting to play, but after school, the only thing I needed was sleep—not rolling toys back and forth. After a while, Terry would pick Billy up and say, "Let him get some rest." And then I'd go back to bed and sleep until dinnertime.

On Friday, I approached one of my classmates, Lydia Mayir and asked how far out of her way Terry's house was.

"Actually, I pass College Road every day to and from school."

"Can I ride with you?" I asked.

"Sure," she said.

Later that day, she spoke to her friend Halina Sulislawski, who also passed College Road every day about sharing the ride.

"OK, I have no problem with that. It's not like we're going out of our way, right?"

"You are right." Lydia agreed.

When Terry picked me up that day, I let her know that I would be riding with Lydia and Halina back and forth to school.

We enjoyed going to school together; we talked about Boolean algebra, logic equations, and numbering systems. We studied together in the library; some days, we stayed late to do our programming assignments together. By the end of the first semester, we had begun to have fun; all the craziness about programs not running right became topics of conversation.

Each time I think about those two girls, I recall that out of sheer naiveté or ignorance, I failed to offer them gas money for riding back and forth to school—it never occurred to me.

A MATTER OF FAITH

On Sundays, I attended church with Terry and her children and then Dr. and Mrs. Ekong picked me up and brought me back to Burlington late in the evening.

One day, we arrived at the Episcopal Church and took our seats in the pew. There were a few members who had sat in the pew got up and changed their position. That dramatic change of places continued until one Sunday night when Terry asked me how I felt about it.

"Obulik, do you feel bad about people changing their seats when we get to church?" she asked, mispronouncing my name.

"No, what do you mean?" I asked.

"I am glad you don't notice."

"Notice what?"

"Don't you notice members changing pews when we arrive at church?"

"What's wrong with that?"

"There is nothing wrong with it, and I'm glad you don't feel bad," she said.

Then she went on to tell me that "when people arrive in America, they do not know how complex this country is. In their own countries, people probably live and worship together. However, in America, some people are biased; they are afraid of associating with other races."

Still confused as to why she was telling me that, she went straight to the point and said, "People change their seats in the church because you're a black man, And they don't want to sit with a black person."

So I realized immediately how uncomfortable going to church with me must have been for her, so I stopped attending church. After all, I did not need to go to church to preserve my relationship with God.

Billy was clinging to me like iron dust to a magnet. He'd not go to sleep unless I tucked him in, and he'd not eat his cereal in the morning unless I fixed it. In fact, every night, Billy would sneak into my room and curl up in my bed while I'd be watching TV in the living room.

"This boy hasn't liked anybody since his father died," Terry would say. "I can't believe how he's attached to Obulik. I'm surprised."

For the most part, my first memorable experience living with Terry was how every time I came out to go to work or school, dogs in the neighborhood would line up, bark, and chase after me.

I recall one afternoon, when I was returning from work, and the dogs were barking and chasing after me, an old lady who lived across the street from Terry's house called out to me.

"Son, come here," she said.

I went over to her, thinking she wanted me to do something for her.

"Yes, ma'am, what can I do for you?" I asked.

"I see the dogs barking at you every time you come out of Terry's house, and so I feel terrible for you. Do you know how to drive?"

"No, ma'am, I do not," I replied.

"Go and learn how to drive," she said. "I have a car for you, so those dogs will stop chasing after you."

After hearing what she said, I ran home fast and told Terry.

"Are you serious?" Terry asked.

"Yes, I am. The old lady said that she feels sorry to see dogs chasing after me."

"Hold on," Terry said. "I will be right back. Let me talk to Miss Wendy."

Terry went over to Miss Wendy's house and came back with a Toyota Corolla and the title. Then she said, "Go and thank Miss Wendy."

Feeling happy, I ran over to Miss Wendy's house and thanked her for the car.

Meanwhile, Terry parked the car in her driveway and made an appointment for my driving lessons, which I took four times, passed the driving test, and got my driver's license.

One day, not too long after I got my license, I received a wedding invitation from my niece Comfort. She was getting married to her longtime boyfriend, Chike. So I was happy, excited and imagined how amazing she'd look walking down the aisle.

On the eve of her wedding, I drove to Bronx, New York, and arrived at her apartment late in the evening while her friends were having a party on the first floor. I heard up in her apartment that the hall at Columbia University was not decorated for the reception. It was like

A MATTER OF FAITH

a kick in the gut, so I wanted to go right away and take care of it, but it was too late at night. The first thing the following morning I went to the hall with a few people and got the reception hall ready for the occasion.

Therefore, I did not see my niece marry in the church. Besides, when I arrived at the reception, the hall was filled with guests, but the food and everything needed to entertain them was back in the Bronx. So I made several trips back and forth to her apartment with a trunk full of party items without help.

For the better part of the wedding, I did nothing but work. Consequently, I missed my niece's wedding and reception. Because of the work, I did during the wedding ceremony in addition to the back and forth driving during the occasion, I felt exhausted. So I left New York and returned to Boston while the reception was still in progress.

Although I did not share in the pleasure of the wedding, I was happy that I was there to prevent the disaster that could have occurred if I had not attended the wedding. So whenever I think of my niece's wedding, I can't help but wonder how shocked she would have felt without me there. I also remembered that her mother always told me to be close to her and wonder if she knew then through maternal instinct that a day like the wedding would come.

Finally, my days in Burlington ended when I transferred to Northeastern University and moved to Boston.

Chapter 2
Always On My Mind

I've been homesick for countries I've never been, and longed to be where I couldn't be.

~ John Cheever

My familiarity with American people began when I was in high school, attending social events at the American Consulate in Enugu, in the Eastern Region of Nigeria. Similarly, my love for America grew from somewhere deep in my soul. No! It was not accidental; not even as a result of watching a spectacularly choreographed rendering of life in the US.

Let me tell you how it happened. America stole my heart on that early afternoon when I was attending the Fourth of July celebration at the American consulate. We were all there—students from various high schools within Enugu, the capital city of the East Region and other invitees seated in the beautiful lawn in front of the consulate dressed up in our school blazers.

Suddenly, a lady, the principal organizer of the consulate's students' social activities distributed pamphlets in which was the preamble of the American Constitution and the American National Anthem.

Before the celebration began; before we sang the American National Anthem, I read the preamble of the American Constitution and fell in love with America instantly.

But it was everything I read in the *Boston Globe* about Boston; after the Nigerian-Biafra war that gave me the mental image or a glimpse into the life in America.

For me, the mystique of Boston lies in the sentiment that sprang up in me after reading about MIT, Harvard University, Northeastern, Boston College, and other universities in the city and felt convinced it

A MATTER OF FAITH

was the education capital of the world. So Boston was always on my mind because to me, Boston was America.

When I moved to Boston — a place that was always on my mind, I was convinced that, I had finally arrived at the place I had dreamed about. I worked at a McDonald's restaurant and for a cleaning company, and I joined a workers union and got health insurance.

My left eye had been damaged when a sharp object hit it—I was a young boy playing in the village square with my mates when it happened. Consequently, I developed cockeye.

One Sunday afternoon, after my health insurance came in the mail, I visited Dr. and Mrs. Ekong, showed them the card, and told Dr. Ekong, "I want to use my health insurance for corrective eye surgery."

"OK, let's do it before school starts," he said. "How many more weeks do you have left before that?"

"Three weeks."

"I will make arrangements for your surgery. How about the coming Friday?" he asked. "You need two weeks off from work."

So I took two weeks off and let Dr. Ekong know that I was ready for Friday.

"I will pick you up at eight o'clock and take you to Mass General," he said. "That's where the procedure will take place, and I will be there during the operation."

On Friday, the day of the operation, Dr. Ekong picked me up and drove to the hospital; he did all the paperwork and took part in the preliminary evaluation.

"The muscle behind the retina is damaged," the operating doctor said. "Straightening it out will do the trick."

After the preliminary evaluation, Dr. Ekong wheeled me to the operation room and asked for local anesthesia. Then the nurse stuck the needle in me and pumped the fluid into my vein. For that reason, I was partially unconscious during the operation, so I could feel the cuts and stitches like gentle scratches—not sharp enough to make me jump up or scream. After the procedure, I lay in the recovery room and waited for the nurse. Instead, Dr. Ekong walked in with a black pad in his hand

and said, "The procedure went very well, so I will take you home. But you have to cover your left eye until you come back for a checkup."

The next day, Mrs. Ekong brought me cold cuts, salad, and vegetables and prepared sandwiches for me before she left. Now the school was about to start, and my checkup appointment was a couple of weeks away, luckily, it was on a Saturday, so it did not interfere with my school activities. On the morning of my appointment, I arrived at the hospital and proceeded to the eye clinic. Then the nurse ushered me into the doctor's office for my checkup. After the usual vital signs verification, the nurse removed my pad, and then the doctor put me through a series of eye tests and told me, "You can stop wearing the eye patch, your eye is OK now."

With a sense of gratitude, I visited Dr. and Mrs. Ekong the following day after church and showed them the result of the procedure.

"They did a good job," Mrs. Ekong said.

"I'd like to thank both of you for your help."

"You don't need to," Mrs. Ekong said. "it gives us a good feeling to watch after you, don't allow your peers to change you."

"I will start work on Monday," I said.

"Be careful," Dr. Ekong said, "stay away from the dust, and cover that eye under the bright light."

Meanwhile, my best friend back in Nigeria, Gabriel Maduka, had arrived in the United States and was living with his brother-in-law in Cambridge, Massachusetts. So one evening, he called me at work and told me, "I have registered for mechanical engineering at Northeastern University too, what do you think about renting an apartment together?"

"There's nothing to think about," I replied, "it is the most commonsense thing to do."

So we rented a two-bedroom apartment on the second floor of Seventy-two Symphony Road, a block away from the school and moved in one week later. Then I changed my work schedule at McDonald's to Saturday and Sunday from eleven PM to seven AM because my classes were between nine o'clock and three o'clock.

Shortly after moving into the apartment, I met two Nigerian students who lived across the street, Rex and Shegu. They too were

A MATTER OF FAITH

students at Northeastern on Nigerian federal scholarships, so we went to school together and became good friends.

One Saturday afternoon, I was sitting on the bench outside my apartment building, reading the *Boston Globe*, when two sexy ladies came out of my apartment building with strollers, two boys, and babies in their arms. For whatever reason, they grabbed my attention, so I went along, walking and chatting with them.

"Where are you two going?" I asked.

"Columbus Avenue," one of them said.

"Why do you want to know?" the other lady asked.

"I would like to help you with the stroller," I replied.

"OK, take one stroller," she said.

Chatting along the way, we walked to the store on Columbus Avenue where they bought what they went there for, and then we walked right back home.

"My name is Ogbuleke Ikebie Ndukwe, and I am from Nigeria," I said.

"I am Jody Marshall," one lady said. "I am from Barbados."

"I am Rosey Davies," the other lady said. "And I am from Trinidad."

Suddenly, a man of average height with broad shoulders unlocked the first-floor apartment door and walked in.

"Daddy, Daddy," the two boys yelled and grabbed him.

"Larry, this is a neighbor on the second floor," Rosey said. "They moved in two weeks ago. This is Larry, my husband."

"I am glad to meet you," I said and shook his hand.

Then the ladies changed the topic immediately to the upcoming carnival.

"I can't wait for the carnival," Rosey said.

"Who's going to watch Pepe and his brother?" Jody asked.

"Larry," Rosey said.

However, I had not heard of the carnival before. So I confessed ignorance of its existence, but still, I was eager to participate as long as Jody and Rosey were in the crowd with me.

When the date of the carnival arrived, Jody and Rosey had their hair and nails done and then at noon, Jody buzzed me up and came to my apartment. Blinded by outright naïveté, I did not realize that she had come deliberately to tease and whip up my raw emotions—judging from how sexy she looked.

"I want to use your mirror," she said. "Rosey is monopolizing hers."

So I pointed to the bathroom and went back to bed.

"Chuks, come and help me with my necklace," she called out.

By that time, I had changed my first name from Ogbuleke to Chuks—my baptismal name so that employers could pronounce it with less difficulty. As I entered the bathroom, she was facing the mirror, and her pantie was down around her ankles.

"Excuse me, I didn't see you are coming," she said and pulled her panties up.

With the necklace around her neck, I secured the hook. Then she stretched her hands backwards and pulled me close to her—real close, and moved her but back and pressed it against my front waistline and then she said, "We will show you how to party tonight." As she turned around to leave, she paused and slapped me tenderly on my cheek, smiling and said "Get ready. We are leaving at two o'clock."

We left at about two o'clock, arrived at Dudley station thirty minutes later, and joined a mosaic of colorful carnival participants enjoying the musical extravaganza. Shortly, trucks and trailers carrying different types of musical instruments began to move in a procession, as Caribbean ethnic music mixed in the air to produce a rare blend of rhythm and beats. So we joined the parade and danced to the music.

Rosey and Jody looked so sexy—quite different from the stroller-pushing ladies I had been walking around the city with. There was a post-carnival party all night; and in that party, they set me on fire with their erotic dancing. "It's all in good fun," Rosey said. "That's what the carnival is about."

For the most part, what made my work at the McDonald's fun was the friends I made. I will never forget four employees who made the most impression on me working there. The first was Watisha Summers,

A MATTER OF FAITH

the second was Eleanor Campbell, the third was Lynette Brown, and the fourth was Jeanette Jack.

Watisha was sexy and provocative, and she loved to flirt and tease; she knew that she had it. One day, I was giving her a ride home from work when suddenly; she wanted to know where I lived, so we stopped by my apartment. She sat on the chair, got up and sat on the desk, and put her legs on my bed.

"What's up with this bed?" she asked.

"Nothing. Why do you want to know?" I asked jokingly.

"Who do you sleep with on this bed?"

"With a girl called Watisha."

"Yeah, you wish," she said.

Summer was winding down, and students who were on co-op were preparing to return to school. One evening, Watisha walked in the store and announced. "I'm leaving for college on Saturday," she hugged everybody in the store. Then she dragged me out of the store and said: "don't sleep on that bed with no other girl in your dream."

Lynette was amicable. We worked well together. After closing on Saturdays, she'd go out to the clubs, and then I'd give her a ride home when the clubs closed.

Eleanor was an Irish girl with blue eyes and blond hair. When I'd be studying in the break room, she'd sit by me and ask questions about computers and math and sometimes about Africa. Mostly, though, I gave her a ride home when we worked the closing shift on Fridays, Saturdays, and Sundays. To other girls, she was my girlfriend, but I did not see it the same way. One day, she came to work and announced that she was quitting to attend Framingham state college.

"I'll come back and work during holidays," she said. Then she hugged me and walked away proudly.

In contrast, I fascinated Jeanette by a few aspects of my African personality, so she hung around me a lot and made my working there more fun.

Most of all, I remember once when I went down to the McDonald's basement to mop the manager's office. As I opened the door, I saw the safe open and full of dollar bills. Sure, the store manager had gone home and left the safe open.

Therefore, I called the store manager, John but he did not answer the call, so I called the regional manager, Mr. Woody and said, "Sir, you've got to come to the store right now."

"Did anybody get shot?" he asked.

"No, sir."

"Are you hurt?"

"No, sir, I am not hurt."

"What is it, then?"

"I can't tell you on the phone," I replied.

"I am in bed with my wife for crying out loud," he said. "Don't call me back. OK?"

"I am so sorry, sir," I apologized.

Next, I checked the doors and made sure they were secured, and then I sat in the office until Woody showed up in the morning; the safe was still open and filled with dollar bills. Finally, after counting the bundles and checking the paperwork, he gave me two weeks off and threw some smirk at me.

✳✳✳

Another incident I will never forget attending Northeastern came one not-so-hot summer evening, I was playing soccer with some Nigerian students on the short street of Symphony Road. Suddenly two ladies parked their car on Hemmingway Street and turned onto Symphony Road—our make-believe soccer field.

As the ladies got out of their car, all six players rushed to talk to the younger one, who they had never met before. I was keeping the goal at the far end, so I just sat there and watched. Then the younger lady pushed the guys aside and beckoned to me to come to her.

"Are you too good to say hi to me?" she asked.

"I don't rush to say hi to people I don't know," I replied.

"OK, could you find us the superintendent of this apartment building?" she asked.

A MATTER OF FAITH

At that moment, I realized I had won her admiration, so I went around the corner and called Mr. Brooks for her. Before they left. She introduced herself and her sister to me. "I am Melba, and this is my sister, Delsey."

Seven days later, while the same group of boys were playing soccer at the same spot as last time, Melba and her sister arrived and asked me to help them move their belongings to the third-floor apartment.

"Come back for dinner," she said as I turned around to leave.

At first, I tried to stay away from Melba because we had just met, and I did not feel comfortable going back for dinner. As a matter of fact, I had few things on my mind at that time; I was looking for a part-time job because I have been dozing off in class for lack of a full night's sleep hence hooking up with a girl was not in my list of things to do.

I must confess, working full time from eleven o'clock at night to seven o'clock in the morning and starting class at nine o'clock, made taking notes in the class hard, so my writing was straight lines up, down, and sideways.

One day I found UPS' advertisement in the *Boston Globe*: it read something like "*people wanted to work four to eight in the evening*" so I thought. "Ah! That's like the ideal job for me." So I drove to Waltham, Massachusetts, and applied. After a short interview, the manager rejected me without giving me any reason.

As a result, I came home, disappointed and upset. Later, Melba came over and asked why I looked depressed. So I explained what had happened. And then like a mother to a child, she said, "Put your clothes on we are going back."

"What's the matter with you?" I asked. "Are you crazy? The man turned me down."

Despite my resistance, she insisted so we drove back to UPS.

"I want to see the manager," she said to the same man who had turned me down about two hours before.

"Yes, I am the manager. Can I help you?" he asked.

"This man works two jobs, and he goes to school full time at the same time," Melba said. "And he came here looking for a job that will enable him to sleep well and go to school without sleeping in the class. I do not think that you will hire anybody more hardworking than him. I am convinced you will like him if you give him the job."

"What is he to you?" he asked.

"He is my friend."

"And who are you?"

"My name is Melba, from Jamaica, and I am spending my vacation here," she said. "We live in the same building."

"OK, I will hire him if he is like what you said. He deserves to go to school without feeling sleepy," the manager agreed and gave me job application and a W-9 form to fill out. Then he said, "You can start on Monday."

At last, we thanked him and went home. Every time Melba and I were together, sparks flew around like bursting fireworks; why wouldn't it—we were two stubborn young friends—the type you can't push around. Still, we enjoyed being together.

One day, Melba came to me while I was coming out of the bathroom with my towel around my waist.

"I am leaving tomorrow. I really don't want to go back, but I am on vacation on a visitor visa, so I can't stay," she said. "I will write to you when I get home."

"You should have told me earlier so I could buy you some gifts."

"You have given me better gifts than anything money could buy."

"OK, I will give you a ride to the airport tomorrow."

"No, it will be hard. I do not want to cry in public. Bye-bye."

"Bye," I replied.

I escorted her to the door and watched her climb the stairs until she vanished behind the third-floor apartment door.

Chapter 3
The Essence of Work-Study

You learn to speak by speaking, to study by studying, to run by running, to work by working; and just so, you learn to love by loving. All those who think to learn in any other way deceive themselves.

~ Saint Francis De Sales

Northeastern University runs a unique system of education, co-operative system [The co-op]. When I applied for admission to Northeastern University, I knew I was heading to an institution that promotes a perfect balance between theory and practice or a well-designed system whence knowledge is enriched through the exercise of what is learned. Besides, what I appreciated most about the co-op was how empowering it could be in the lives of students who dared to apply themselves. So I was determined to use my time well.

> **Learning is progressive and systematic acquisition of knowledge, but it is the successful exercise of what is learned that defines the value of the knowledge acquired.**

The co-op works like this: Students spend twelve months of their freshman and senior years in school—no summer holidays, and no slacking off. In fact, one could say with a certain measure of conviction that it was never intended to be a slack place. The three years in between are split between the classroom and the co-op.

Consequently, when I finished my freshman year and three months of my sophomore year, I was ready for the co-op. During that time, students were being sent out for interviews.

Although I had not been invited for co-op interview yet, I was hopeful that I would be. After all, it was Christmas season—the most optimistic time of the year. So I decided that I'd not worry about the co-op until after the new year celebration.

At first, I resigned myself to spending the Christmas alone after my best friend and roommate, Gabriel, had gone to Cambridge to spend Christmas with his sister and brother-in-law at MIT—on that chilly Christmas Eve. Then suddenly, I received a phone call from Mrs. Ekong.

"We are expecting you," she said.

"I wasn't sure you'll be home."

"Doctor is on call, but I don't have to go to work until Monday of next week," she said. "Get in the car and bring your ass over here. We are having light entertainment by the fireplace."

Arriving in Newton, they were playing light music and helping themselves to all kinds of drinks, so I joined in and had some Pepsi and cookies. Then the following morning—the Christmas day, I woke up very early as always and helped the maid with house chores. And feeling eager to go to church with Dr. and Mrs. Ekong, and then something happened: after a shower, I put my clothes on, went to the bathroom to comb my hair, and smelled myself— the first time ever that happened. I was ashamed to tell the maid, so I hid in the guest room until Dr. Ekong came for me.

"We are waiting for you," he said.

"I can't go with you," I replied subdued and ashamed.

"What happened to you?"

"I smelled myself."

"Did you put on deodorant after your shower?" He inquired.

"No, I forgot to."

"Now you know why deodorant is the most popular item in the market today," he said. "Everybody smells if they don't put it on. Come on, put it on and let's go."

Feeling relieved by what he said, I put the deodorant on and went to church. Still, I kept sniffing my armpits all day to check whether the odor had come back as embarrassment and insecurity haunted me. Then

A MATTER OF FAITH

coming home, I went straight to the bathroom and put some more deodorant on my armpits, fearing the obnoxious odor could come back.

Nevertheless, we had a very joyful Christmas. We watched Christmas specials on TV and drank eggnog.

On the first day of school after the New Year, I learned that Arthur D. Little, a software company in Cambridge, had invited me for a co-op interview. So I sharpened my skill in some programming languages I had learned such as Cobol, Fortran, Pascal, and Assembly.

When I arrived for the interview, I filled out application forms and got ready. Then the chief engineer, Mr. Ben Gordon, walked in, went to his office, and came back to the lobby.

"Are you…from Northeastern?" he asked, unable to say my name.

"Yes, sir, my name is Ogbuleke," I said.

"Follow me, please," he said.

I followed him to his office.

"Have a seat," he said. "Have you taken Fortran?"

"Yes, I have, sir."

"OK, how would you code this simple problem in Fortran?"

Stretching his hand across his desk, he gave me the question paper, a pen, and a blank sheet. When I finished coding the program, he went to the computer room and compiled the code. Then he came back and looked at me over the top of his eyeglasses.

"Well, it is a good start. Let's see what the output looks like," Gordon said, and then he went back to the computer room.

"It looks like you did the job," he said. "The code worked."

After the practical test, Ben gave me a brief overview of what the company was working on. Then he said, "hold on, I'll be right back," and went to his secretary's office. Now I had the urge to visit the men's room, so I followed to go to the men's room. Then I heard him say to the secretary, "I'd like to hire this guy, but I can't pronounce his name."

After hearing that, I went back to his office, called the International Students Office at Northeastern University immediately, and requested a name change.

"Good morning, sir. My name is Ogbuleke Ikebie Ndukwe. I'm about to get an offer for a co-op job," I said. "But my name is creating a problem. I would like to change my first name immediately."

"What would you like your alias to be?" he asked.

"I would like it to be my baptismal name, Chuks sir." "C"-"h"-"u"-"k"-"s," I said and spelled it slowly.

"Consider it done," he said.

When Ben came back to his office, I told him that I had changed my first name while he was in the secretary's office.

"What did you change it to?" he asked.

"I changed it to Chuks so you won't have any problem pronouncing it."

"How do you pronounce it?"

"You can pronounce it as Chucks or Chooks."

"That's great," he said, "how did you come up with that name so fast?"

"It's my baptismal name," I replied.

"Splendid, you can think fast on your feet," he said.

After the interview, Ben told me, "We have a large database of Fortran codes that need to be modified. So you'll be working with me during your co-op period to do that. You can start on Monday. Congratulations!" Then his secretary escorted me to the door and said. "See you on Monday."

With my change of name in mind, I reported to the dean's office the next day to make sure his office changed my first name as I requested.

"Good morning, sir. My name is Ogbuleke Ikebie Ndukwe," I said. "I called you yesterday from Arthur D. Little in Cambridge when I was close to losing my co-op job offer."

"Yes, we made the necessary changes yesterday," he said. "But at some point, you have to execute an affidavit of change of name with a federal judge. For now, you can use the new name as an alias."

Although my interview went very well, still I was aware of the possibility of screwing up, so I went to work on Monday feeling insecure.

A MATTER OF FAITH

For the most part, I assisted Ben in modifying routines of existing libraries of Fortran codes, compiled and ran each modified piece of software code, and attached the output to the print copy.

Meanwhile, I could no longer work at both UPS and Arthur D. Little, so I quit the UPS job. Aside from working on the codes, I followed Ben around the office and assisted him with everything he had to do in the computer room—to learn the trick of the trade.

During this first co-op, I worked at Arthur D. Little for three months modifying codes, assisting Ben around the computer room, and filing printouts. On a few occasions, we had lunch at his favorite Irish restaurant and chatted about some of the professors at Northeastern University.

After our brief chat, I realized that he was an alumnus of Northeastern University. And knowing that he understood the essence of my co-op in his office, I relaxed and enjoyed my work. At the end of the chat, he told me to put my stack of codes away.

"Let's go to lunch," he said.

"It is not the time for lunch, sir," I said.

"Don't worry. Let's go," Mr. Gordon ordered.

We arrived at a small Irish restaurant not far from the office. Then Ben ordered rib-eye and mashed potatoes.

"What is your pleasure?" he asked.

"Hamburger and French fries," I answered.

"We don't serve hamburgers here," the cook said.

"They serve good food here. Check the menu and make your choice," Ben said.

"OK, give me corned beef and mashed potatoes," I said.

"There you go," Ben said.

The cook came back with Pepsi-Colas as if he knew what we wanted.

"I've come here every day for six years," Ben said. "I can sit here without a word and have my food on the table."

On the day my co-op ended, I had a meeting with Ben in his office during which he said, "You are a good kid. I have enjoyed working with you. I will transmit my official appraisal of your performance to the university, and I have to tell you what will not be in that official document. Every manager loves an employee who is dependable, helpful, and diligent, and you have all those qualities. I will ask for you to come back during your next co-op period."

Returning to school the following Monday, Gab and I registered for courses that would allow us to go to school together although we split to different halls when we got to school; he was one year ahead of me and majoring in a different field. Some days I took a detour to the cafeteria to check out the specials for the day to decide in advance whether or not I'd go home for lunch.

Generally, the school was going well; I was not dozing off during lectures anymore, and my notes looked solid—an improvement I could only credit to a full night's sleep.

Three months passed by quickly, and I was back at the co-op at Arthur D. Little. Ben had taken on program simulation to determine the logical results of the code we had been compiling given the appropriate inputs.

But for me, I continued the work I was doing previously. Mostly though, I just watched Ben and marveled at the contrast between the work I did as an electrical supervisor—back in Nigeria and the work of software engineer. And while I reveled in the office culture, I was also keenly conscious that I had a long way to go before I'd be competent enough to do what Ben was doing. Suddenly Ben popped the question:

"Do you plan on going back to Africa after your graduation?"

"Yes, I do sir."

"Can you find a job as a software engineer when you go back?"

"There might be opportunities by that time," I answered.

"If you can't find a job there, would you like to come back and work for me?"

"Yes, thank you, sir."

"If you keep on at this rate, you will do fine in this profession," he said.

On Wednesday afternoon, Ben called a meeting and addressed the employees.

A MATTER OF FAITH

"Arthur D. Little will not be here in three months," he said. "However, we've signed another contract with another company in Mansfield, Massachusetts."

According to Ben, Mansfield was about a one-hour drive from Cambridge. I could not hide my disappointment while Ben was speaking because I had hoped to do all of my co-ops at Arthur D. Little, but that hope fizzled after the meeting. Finally, my co-op ended on Friday, with a meeting Ben and I had at lunch at his favorite Irish restaurant.

"Today is your last day with us," he said. "I will transmit your appraisal to the university as usual. But I'm not certain about our existence here in the future, because our contract is expiring. However, I have enjoyed working with you and learning a little bit about Nigeria. It's only three o'clock; you can leave anytime you choose."

✳ ✳ ✳

After that meeting, I left the office around three o'clock and drove along the Charles River just to watch the seagulls' acrobatic maneuver in the water. When I got home, I went straight to Rosey's house.

"What happened? You look like you did not get some from that tramp I saw coming out of your apartment?" she said.

"What tramp? I'm just getting home from work."

"Looks like you played hooky to be with that tramp with blue eyes and blond hair."

"That girl happens to be my girlfriend," I said. "You must stop calling her a tramp."

Meanwhile, Jody had come over and was preparing hamburgers and French fries. Rosey's kids woke up, and they were excited to see me, so I played with them until Rosey served us the food. Surprisingly, I felt better after eating and wrestling with Rosey's kids—Pepe and Damian.

"Bring out that deck of cards your Irish girlfriend gave you," Rosey said.

I brought the cards out and pulled my chair close to the table. I was ignorant of card games and really sucked at it; I could shuffle, but that was all I could do, so they beat me mercilessly.

"You're a sorry-ass player," Jody said. Then they left.

Now Gab came home and did not have better news either. He was not sure that he would be going back to his co-op job. So we were in a funk that evening.

On Christmas Eve, Dr. and Mrs. Ekong stopped by on their way to a concert at the Boston Symphony Hall—one block away from my apartment to let me know that they were expecting me the following day. So the next morning, I went to Newton and spent Christmas with Dr. and Mrs. Ekong.

Conscious of the moment I smelled myself the previous Christmas, I made sure I had my deodorant with me. On Christmas Day, we attended church together. Then in the evening, Dr. and Mrs. Ekong entertained guests with me bartending, while the maid served food. After the guests had left, I told Dr. and Mrs. Ekong that "I have changed my first name to Chuks,"

"That's smart because your name is hard to pronounce," Mrs. Ekong said.

"That was my reason for doing so," I said.

When I went back to school on Monday, I felt less confident about the possibility of finding another software company for my next co-op. Still, most of the courses I registered for were software programming languages as if to prepare for another co-op. Now the quarter was ending, and students were attending interviews for co-op.

One day, I got a note to attend an interview at TeleAudit in Bedford, Massachusetts. So I did, and got hired, and came home happy. Gab came back in the evening happy too.

"I'm going back to my job," he said.

The quarter ended, and then we went back to co-op.

Chapter 4
Software Then Hardware

Computers themselves, and software yet to be developed, will revolutionize the way we learn

~ Steve Jobs

The first things I noticed upon my arrival at TeleAudit for the interview was the large laboratory and people who sat by their workbench—all absorbed in their work. After the meeting, I got the job, and in a moment, I thought, "Bedford is far from Boston by my estimation, and my car? No! It will not endure the stress of heavy travel.

Also, I remembered that my car, Toyota Corolla had been a gift, so I decided to give it to a friend rather than sell it for money or even use it for a down payment on another car.

For this reason, I attempted to give it to my friend, Rex Kanu. But Rex did not have a driver's license; he was on a scholarship and did not have any need to go anywhere—beyond school, which was two blocks away from his apartment building. Finally, I gave the car to an auto mechanic and bought another vehicle, a Dodge Charger.

When I arrived at TeleAudit on my first day of work, the office was still locked, so I waited until the secretary, Miss MaryAnn, arrived. Then we had breakfast in the cafeteria—tea and toast—before the other workers came, and little did I know that tea and toast—for breakfast would become our daily ritual throughout my co-op invitation there.

Now Mr. Jack Brown arrived and introduced me to his engineers: John, Glen, and Pat. One hour later, two gentlemen in suits Mr. Jimmy Olsen and Tim McNeil—consulting engineers arrived. A few minutes later, Mr. Jack said, "John, let Shoots play with the test fixture until I decide what his assignment will be."

Getting the test fixture from John, I played with it for a while—until lunchtime, to be exact and then after lunch, I asked for the schematics, test procedure, and studied them until closing. The following day, I connected the fixture to a printed circuit board and began to play with it like a toy. I turned switches on and off one at a time and recorded the light pattern in my notebook—in a binary mode. Then after lunch, I began to decode the binary to hexadecimal as Mr. Jack stood behind me for a few minutes and called out to John, "John, take a look at what Shoots is doing." This time I said, "Sir, you got my name wrong again, you can pronounce it as Chooks or Chucks." Then he apologized.

Now John came over and checked my notebook. Then he turned to Mr. jack and said, "That's great, I was getting ready to give him a tutorial on the test setup and procedure."

"Looks like we've found a technician to assist Pat," Mr. Jack said. "Well, Chuks, congratulations. You've got yourself a permanent position for your co-op."

Although not expected to know much yet, I worked with the engineers for three months, checking, testing, and assembling printed circuit boards until one day, when Mr. Jack invited me to his office just before lunch.

"Mr. Chuks, this is the last day of your co-op with us," he said. "We've enjoyed working with you. It is hard to believe that you have been here for only three months. It feels like you have been working here forever. My engineers like your work ethic. In fact, they would like you to stay, and I feel the same way. I hope that you have enjoyed yourself enough to want to come back in three months."

"Sir, I would love to come back," I said.

At the end of the day, MaryAnn gave me a coffee mug I enjoyed drinking tea with while having breakfast with her during my subsequent co-op invitations.

"You would not believe how much the engineers like you," she said. "We've had quite a few students from your school, and the engineers never liked any of them, but this time they can't stop talking about how you came in and grabbed the bull by the horns. I will miss having early-morning tea with you. Good luck in school."

A MATTER OF FAITH

On Saturday, I was tired and had no intention of going out. The weather was not particularly pleasant, and I had forgotten that Melba had arrived in Boston the previous day. Suddenly, my door-bell went off, and then I buzzed the visitor in. When I opened the door, I saw Melba walking up the stairs, so I ran forward to hug her and heard my apartment door slam shut behind me. Indeed, I had locked us out. Now standing there in the hallway—amused by what I just did, Melba jeered.

"Serves you right," she said.

"What do you mean by that?" I asked.

"The first time we met, your friends rushed to greet me; instead you kept cool like a tough guy," she said. "To watch, you rush to greet me and lock yourself out of your apartment is a fitting payback. Let's go to my sister's house."

"Who brought you here?" I asked.

"My sister is waiting downstairs to make sure you are home before she takes off."

"I can't go out in my pajamas."

"You still got your car, right?"

"Yes, I do."

"OK, we will be in a car, so nobody will see you in pajamas."

"My car key is inside," I said.

Meanwhile, Gab arrived and unlocked the door, and then Melba let her sister know that I was home.

"Come on, take me on a ride in that car," she said. "I know you bought it to impress your girl."

So we drove down Columbus Avenue to Route 93 turned right to Route 128 and then Route 9 and back.

"I love that car," she said. And then we went inside my apartment and rekindled the fire we left smothering inside of us after she had gone home the first time and distance kept us apart. So we enjoyed the evening together before I took her home.

One day I was on the computer trying to type in my code; it seemed like endless work. Yes! I had not taken typing lessons nor learned how to use the keyboard—strange for a student whose passion was computer programming. In fact, only trade school students learned how to type when I was growing up and in high school. Then at Northeastern, I had registered for typing classes once, but when I entered the hall on the first day of class and saw girls everywhere in the class, and chatting loudly, I turned around and walked out.

As my software programming progressed, I had sat in front of a computer and regretted my action.

Ashamed of my inability to operate the keyboard efficiently, I came up with a scheme to hide it. I went to the computer room every night, when no student was around, I pecked on the keyboard and typed in my code—a brilliant plan to avoid being laughed at. Then during school hours, I joined my classmates in the computer room to debug my code without exposing myself to ridicule.

On Monday, the professor gave the class a computer programming assignment due on Friday. I went home, wrote the algorithm, and did the coding the following day. Then on Wednesday after classes, I went to the computer room at night—when not many students were around and pecked in my code. On Thursday afternoon, I began to debug the code. By typing in my code slowly at night, I proudly worked on the computer during the day like students who did not have typing inabilities.

Now I had finished debugging and compiling the code, and everything seemed to be going according to plan. But when I ran it, the result did not come out entirely correct. So I began to look for the cause of the incorrect output. "Could it be poor logic in my code?" I wondered.

Still wondering, I ran to the printer to get my printout and coming back the screen was blank—my code deleted and now came the dilemma—a serious one, at that. I could hand in my assignment and get partial credit for the error-free code. However, how much I would be penalized for the incorrect result, I could not guess.

Therefore, I had to reenter the code. God knows it was the last thing I would do in front of other students. So, I took the printout home to figure out why the output was not correct before reentering the code. Next, I did a manual run on the computational loop and discovered I did not initialize the computational loop properly. Late that evening, after dinner and a short rest, I went back to the computer room to peck in my code.

First, I arrived at the computer room, sat down in front of the computer, and glanced both ways to make sure nobody was looking. Second, I began to peck at the keyboard. Shame or no shame, I could not have cared less. Nevertheless, on my right, one girl was pointing at me, laughing. I guess she found my typing inability amusing.

"Hey, I haven't taken typing courses yet," I said. "If you help me by typing in my code, I will help you debug yours."

"Are you sure?" She asked.

"A hundred percent sure," I said.

So she came over, sat down, and within minutes, she finished typing in my code.

"There you go," she said.

Then she brought her printout over to my desk, and looking at it, her algorithm was nothing like mine.

"Why don't we compile my code first?" I said. "If it compiles error-free, then you can replace yours with mine."

"OK," she nodded in agreement.

To convince her that I was a programming genius, we did a manual run on the code again while I recorded the data we expected to get at the output. Finally, we finished the exercise and got the correct output.

"You are really good at this stuff," Erika said. "I didn't even know what I was doing."

"Let's run it before you shower me with compliments," I said.

With the previous incident—when I lost my code still fresh in my mind, we ran the code twice and got the correct output. And then we printed the last version of everything. Then I said, "Why don't you enter your code so we can run it as well?"

"Great idea," she said.

Then she took over and typed in her code, which compiled error-free, and then we ran it and got the correct output.

"By the way, my name is Chuks who sucks at the computer keyboard," I said.

"I am Erika Jones who sucks at computer programming," she said jokingly and I laughed. And then she continued, "that's two sucking people who finished their assignments on time, maybe the two sucking people should work together often and help each other out, so nobody will know they suck."

Then I escorted her to her dormitory before I went home.

Meanwhile, Dr. Ekong had been offered a job in Rolling Hills, California, and Saturday was Dr. Ekong and his family's departure date, so I drove to Newton, Massachusetts, to say good-bye to his family.

When the quarter ended. I was back at work at TeleAudit, and nothing had changed: MaryAnn was in her office; Mr. Jack was in his office, and the engineers were joking around in the lab.

MaryAnn followed me to the lab, and the engineers gathered around.

"We missed you, Chuks," MaryAnn said. "We had another student after you, but he was a joke. I know Jack would be happy to see you back."

"Let's welcome the real engineering student back to the lab," John said.

"Yeah, welcome back, man!" Pat said as the engineers cheered, and we embraced each other like soccer players who had just scored a winning goal in the world cup match.

As if he heard my voice, Mr. Jack came out of his office and joined the guys in the lab.

"Good morning, sir," I greeted him.

"How are you, Chuks?" He inquired. "It's good to see you back."

"I was just telling him about Mike," MaryAnn said.

"It's true," Jack said without hesitation. "I asked for another student to replace you after you went back to school. In response, the university sent Mike, and I can't tell what he did for the three months he was here."

"Can anybody tell?" Pat joked.

"Mike did not even know what we do here," John said. "I couldn't stand him."

"Aren't white students supposed to be smarter than black students?" Glen asked jokingly, and everybody dispersed.

A MATTER OF FAITH

After this friendly welcome, I waited impatiently for an assignment, hoping John would give me something different this time but he did not say anything. Therefore, I went over to his corner and asked for a job.

"Come on, man, you still got the VIP seat; same as before," he said.

At that instant, I took my seat beside Pat as usual and began to tidy up the test bench.

"Hey, Pat, move over or visit the men's room. I want to straighten out the test area," I said. "It has lost its luster."

"I don't have to move over. Let's do it," Pat said, "we have enough orders to last throughout your co-op period."

"Are we going to be traveling to deploy the systems?"

"No, they've trained four guys to deploy the systems while we focus on producing them," Pat said.

Pat and I resumed the printed-circuit-board-testing after cleaning the test area. As Pat had said, we had enough boards to test throughout my co-op period.

In many ways, my experience back in Nigeria made it easy for me to embrace the work culture and blend in with the engineers. On my way to work the following day, traffic on Route 93 north was bumper to bumper owing to a fatal accident in which two people died and caused a long traffic jam. So getting to work, I was two hours late.

"Chuks, what happened?" MaryAnn asked as if she did not hear about the accident. "I missed you at breakfast this morning."

"Traffic was bad on Route 93," I said. "We sat on the Boston overpass for an hour and a half without any movement."

"It could have been worse," she said.

"Did you get lost, man?" John teased.

"No, I know my way pretty well," I said.

"I thought he went back to Africa," Glen joked.

Mr. Jack came to my aid as a series of rapid mockery, but welcoming remarks came at me. "There was a fatal accident on Route 93 that caused traffic to backed up all the way to the city," he said.

~ 33 ~

"I was worried about you when I heard on the radio this morning that two people died in a car crash on Route 93," MaryAnn said. "I know that you take route 93 to work, and you drive fast too."

Stunned by MaryAnn's comment about my fast driving habit, I began to watch the speedometer while driving.

Gab was finishing his senior year and had completed his final examinations; yearbook photos were taken and Gab had written his family to let them know the date of his return to Nigeria.

I came home before Gab one day and had begun to cook dinner when suddenly, the door swung open.

"The final exam results are out, and I am graduating!" Gab screamed.

"Congratulations, man!"

"Let's go to the bar. I want to get drunk," he said. "You can have Pepsi and get us back safely."

"I have to eat first. I am hungry," I said. "You have to wait until I finish."

When I finished eating, we walked a few blocks to a bar on Massachusetts Avenue and there he had a few drinks, and I had Pepsi. We hung around the bar until Gab began to lose his coordination, and then we went home.

Getting home, I helped him get upstairs and in his bed. A few weeks later, Gab graduated. And finally, on the day of his departure, I escorted him to Logan International Airport, where he boarded the plane back to Nigeria.

Beyond the anxiety of losing my best friend, the burden of keeping the apartment, and the difficulty of finding somebody—the type I'd like to share the apartment with occupied my mind.

So I posted "Roommate Wanted" signs in Laundromats and campus notice boards. As a result, a few people came to look at the apartment and brought their loud friends, which in itself scared the hell out of me. Regardless, my neighbor Rosey and I interviewed several applicants but gave up after a few weeks of trying when I realized, that living with a total stranger might undermine my simple way of living—few visitors and reasonable noise.

A MATTER OF FAITH

As my co-op was winding down, I began to have more fun joking with the engineers while testing printed circuit boards and felt confident that I had become adept in testing not only the printed circuit boards but also the systems. On the final day of my co-op period, Mr. Jack and I had an informal chat in his office as we enjoyed cookies and Pepsi Cola. Then he began his usual send-off speech:

"Mr. Chuks today is the day you and I usually get together and chat about your co-op period and what I think about your performance," he said. "But this time is different. I have nothing to say except to wish you luck in school and to let you know that we expect to see you back next period. You can leave anytime you wish. I have already forwarded the required evaluation to the university."

After that short send-off speech, I hung around with the engineers and MaryAnn for a while and then I left the office.

I went back to school on Monday, and I was now in my junior year. I registered for advanced electronic, field theory, artificial intelligence, and economics. Then I met Rex and Shegu on my way home, turned around, and went back to school with them. After registering their courses, we stopped at the auditorium and played table tennis, which I am not proud to say that for the several rounds we played, both of them beat me really badly.

In that quarter of school, my favorite Professors stuffed my brain with transistor and field theory, and so I could not wait for the quarter to end; I had heard enough. Nevertheless, it was not until the end of the quarter after I had gone back to the co-op that I realized the importance of the courses I had just taken.

For me, the end of that quarter was the beginning of a period of anxiety because I had not planned to return to Nigeria after graduation, and life had become a little uncertain.

When I arrived at TeleAudit for my final co-op, MaryAnn was opening the office door, so we exchanged pleasantries and had breakfast as always.

"It's good to see you back," she said.

"Likewise, MaryAnn," I replied.

As we were leaving the cafeteria, the whole crew arrived at the same time.

"How was school?" Pat asked.

"OK, I guess."

"The system has been selling like hotcakes, so we have been busy since you went back to school," Pat said.

"We are processing more orders," MaryAnn added.

To be honest, I was glad to know that the company was doing well and that my job was secure for three months.

But looking around, I did not see Jimmy and Tim, so I asked, "What happened to Jimmy and Tim?"

"They are designing a computer at the company Mr. Keagan started in Andover," MaryAnn said.

Soon Mr. Jack arrived.

"Good morning, sir," I greeted him.

"Good morning, Chuks. How are you?" he inquired.

"I am very well, sir. Thank you," I said.

Just as MaryAnn and I were entering the office on Monday, a truck rolled into the parking lot; the driver got out and asked for directions to the TeleAudit shipping dock to drop off a carton containing a system that caught fire in the field. So MaryAnn showed the driver where to drop off the container—on the receiving platform.

Later in the afternoon, Mr. Jack ordered the carton open to see how much damage the system—inside the container sustained. The system had been in operation for a while and caught fire for an unknown reason. Looking at it, we saw that it was severely damaged from how smoky it looked. Then Mr. Jack said, "We have to ship another system to replace it right away."

At that moment, another system was sitting in the lab, so we put it in the carton, and rolled it to the shipping bay then a truck picked it up later and carried it away.

"I have to wait for the police report on that system before I decide what to do with it," Mr. Jack said.

Meanwhile, I walked around the burned system several times and wondered what could have started the fire and the extent of the damage it sustained.

A MATTER OF FAITH

✻ ✻ ✻

After receiving the police report, Mr. Jack ordered Pat to check the system and see whether we could salvage any of the parts. Immediately and without thinking or even letting Mr. Jack finish his statement, I jumped out of my seat and told Mr. Jack that I could get the system to work again.

"What did you say, Chuks?" Mr. Jack asked.

"I can get that system to work again," I repeated.

"I want you to take a good look at it," he said, "and let me know at the end of the day whether you still think you can fix it."

Remarkably, what surprised me thinking about it later, was not that I wanted to repair the system but my hold-on-I-am-here spontaneous reaction. No, that wasn't my first time; I remember reacting in the same manner far back in my sixth grade when I turned on an electric light on in a dark classroom and shouted with the same spontaneity "I want to become an electrical engineer when I grow up."

I attracted everybody's attention in the lab. Notably, Glen—I could see him shaking his head.

"You are joking, right?" Pat asked.

"No, I am not joking," I said.

"If you get that system to work again," John said, "consider yourself an engineer."

Afterwards, Mr. Jack came in the lab, walked around the system a few times, and then he came to my desk and asked, "Chuks, have you thought about your request?"

"Yes, sir, I am serious," I replied.

"OK, that system is all yours," he said. "If you get it to work again, I will put you on the payroll as a full-time engineer. That means that you can consider yourself hired by TeleAudit."

I cannot say that I was confident of success. However, I drew comfort from the power of *the fear of failure*. I went to work on Monday and began to work on the system by wiping off the frame with cleaning fluid so I could see the system inside and outside clearly. Next, I extracted the power cabinet, cleaned it up, and put it away.

On Tuesday, I began to extract the boards from the system and stored them in a bin for visual inspection, and then I cleaned the empty cabinet and let everything dry for a couple of days.

I had gotten the frame to look like new by Friday then I began to check each board visually and put it away for further on-the-bench testing.

The following Monday, I began to test each board and labeled those that passed the test "good" and those that failed "bad." While checking the boards, I found the board that caused the fire and put it aside for further inspection and then I continued to test the rest. After examining all the boards, the full extent of the problem I was dealing with became evident.

The fire had started in one board and went up to the angle iron along with the wiring. First, I rewired the frame. Then I put the system through a safety test, that lasted for two days which the system passed.

At this juncture, I had only three weeks left before the end of my co-op period. So I worked a little bit faster; I put the power cabinet back in the frame and conducted another test with the power supply in operation. Coming back to that board that caused the fire, I simply replaced it with a new board.

One week before my last day, I got the system ready for hand-off to Mr. Jack. At first, I was afraid to turn it on, but I overcame my fears, powered it up, and let it run for two hours. Then I ran the final system test and let the system run for three hours. At that moment, I had a warm and fuzzy feeling from how well the system started without red, yellow, or flashing light—it passed the test.

On Monday, after putting my toolbox away, I informed Mr. Jack that I had restored the system back to its fully functional condition, and handed the system over to him. Then he called John to his office and said, "I want you to test Chuks' system thoroughly for one full day, and let me have the result before Wednesday."

Before the closing time on Tuesday, John gave Mr. Jack the test result. Then we met in his office and enjoyed Pepsi-Cola and cookies.

A MATTER OF FAITH

"That's an amazing job, Chuks," he said. "Consider yourself one of my engineers."

Finally, after lunch on Wednesday, I joined Mr. Jack in Mr. Keagan's office. He was the founder and president of TeleAudit.

"I heard about the system that went up in smoke," Mr. Keagan said. "Jack, what is the status of that system?"

"I was about to dismantle the frame and salvage what we could," Mr. Jack said. "But Chuks challenged me and said that he could get it to work again. I did not believe him at first, but he insisted, then I allowed him to work on it. I did not have any expectation of seeing the system functional again. But yesterday he completed the repair, John tested it all day, and it works like new. I promised Chuks that I would hire him as an engineer if he restored the system, which he has done, so I recommend him for a full-time position as an electrical engineer."

"There is no doubt that Chuks has made himself noticed during his time here," Mr. Keagan said. "From today forward, Chuks can come to work anytime he doesn't have classes, and we will pay him as an engineer. Jimmy and Tim are working in Andover at Spectrametrics, a new company I started last year. I would like Chuks to work with them so he can learn computer design and support their efforts."

After that meeting, I filled out some forms and returned them to MaryAnn. Then later, Mr. Jack invited me to his office and gave me a company ID tag, the address, and telephone number of Spectrametrics in Andover, Massachusetts.

"You can leave anytime you wish today so you can rest for a few days before school begins," he said.

"Didn't I tell you that Mr. Keagan was interested in you?" MaryAnn asked.

"Yes, you did, but I did not believe it."

"He talks about your potential, and he is right," MaryAnn said. "You have exceeded everyone's expectations by far. I know that you will be working in Andover most of the time, but you should stop by the office sometimes, and when your wife gets here, don't fail to let me know."

"Good-bye, MaryAnn."

"Bye, Chuks," she replied.

I recognized that I would never come back to TeleAudit on co-op; that was it. Nevertheless, I was leaving on friendly terms, and I would always be a welcome visitor. As a final act, I shook the engineers' hands, got in my car, and took off. I could have been flying, but traffic on Route 93 was bumper to bumper, so I went with the flow.

On Monday, Rex, Shegu, and I registered our courses, and then we played table tennis before leaving the campus. We were seniors now and looking forward to graduating together.

For me, the co-op had been a huge success; I could not think of any other student who was walking around with a company ID tag and already employed as an engineer going into his or her senior year. I do not claim to have been anyway as smart as any other student. However, it is undeniable that by all accounts, I applied myself well, to the recognition of my co-op employer.

During the first week of school, there was not much happening during the first week of classes, so on Tuesday, I went to Andover to see what Spectrametrics looked like and what Jimmy and Tim were working on.

I drove around Andover for a while before finding Spectrametrics at last, then I discovered that Jimmy and Tim were not in the lab, but their engineering aide, Russ, was there, looking at a large sheet of paper.

"Hi, my name is Chuks I. Ndukwe," I said. "Mr. Keagan told me that I'll be working here with Jimmy and Tim."

"Yeah, you are the guy from Bedford. I am Russ," he said. "Your desk is over there." He pointed at a desk by the corner.

"When do you expect Jimmy and Tim in the office?"

"They come in when they choose. Some days they work from their home offices," he said. "You can start by looking through the schematics over there. I guess that's what you will be working on."

I arrived at work on Thursday as Tim was in the laboratory drawing schematics, and Russ was separating electronic parts.

"Have you guys met?" Tim asked.

"Yes, Chuks came to work on Tuesday," Russ said.

A MATTER OF FAITH

"Let's go to the conference room," Tim said. "I want to show you what Spectrametrics is all about."

Jimmy and Tim were designing a computer for the system—Spectrometer the company was working on.

"Don't worry about how all these parts work," he said. "That will come later. These are schematics, and the other two are the assembly—front and back; concentrate on understanding the assembly drawing. They show how you will be connecting the parts on the schematics. And if you run into trouble, I'll help you with any questions you may have."

Tim had completed four pages of the schematic drawings with two more to go. Although I was familiar with the schematic diagram, still, the symbols in his drawings were well over my head. Therefore, I began to doubt my ability to do the job.

"How are you feeling?" he had inquired once.

"I'm going to need lots of help," I said.

"You got it," he replied.

Notably, the electronic revolution was underway; the vacuum tubes—diodes, triodes, and so on—manufactured by Raytheon, Western Electric, and others were being replaced by semiconductors—chips, ICs, and transistors manufactured by Fairchild, Motorola, and Sony, which had introduced transistor radios already.

When lectures began on Monday, Rex, Shegu, and I were taking advanced courses in materials, so we attended classes together. I had one class on Wednesdays and Fridays at nine o'clock, so I went to work after class—on those days.

On Wednesday, Jimmy arrived at the lab grinning and greeted me with, "What's going on, Chuks?"

"I am trying to understand these drawings," I said.

"Don't worry. You will be fine."

Then after a cup of coffee, he came over to my desk and walked me through the drawings. He kept referring to off-sheet and in-sheet signals, but I did not see any lines or traces with those names.

Later in the afternoon, after Jimmy had left, I told Tim that I did not see the traces Jimmy referred to as off-sheet and in-sheet. "Can you show me those signals?" I asked. Then Tim explained the meaning of the expressions to me.

One day, I arrived at work in the afternoon and saw a big sign on the door next to the lab: *"DANGER DO NOT ENTER"* additionally a coaxial cable lay on the rug from that room, down the hallway, and out to the entrance.

By that time, I had taken advanced courses on field theory so that configuration did not make much sense to me; in fact, it was at odds with the textbook.

Now the quarter was ending, and we were taking our final examinations, so I did not go to work for two weeks. After the exams, I went to work every day until the beginning of the second quarter. I had chosen my courses carefully so that they fell within the morning hours, that way, I went to work in the afternoon.

When I went to work one day, Tim had set up a workbench and two high chairs by the bench. He sat on one of the chairs with a perforated board, a roll of thin wire, and a few tools on the workbench.

"This is our workbench," Tim said to me. "I will show you what to do with this board."

He gave me two assembly drawings. The first with parts placed on one side, and the second—the reverse side of the same board, with cobwebs of wires twisted on thin pegs.

"Take your time and study how the parts are placed," he said.

I looked at the drawings over and over again, and the only thing I grasped was that one large part was at the center with other components surrounding it. I could not tell why that was the case or whether they were in any order.

So I kept studying the drawings until he called me to the workbench again and explained the layout.

"This is how the parts you see on the schematics are placed," he said. "Watch how I'll replicate the layout."

He placed the central piece—the socket, first and the others around it. As he was putting the chips, I noticed that he placed each chip close to other chips connected to it and the chips had markings on one end.

When Tim finished the placement, he took the assembly drawing from me and compared it with his work.

A MATTER OF FAITH

"What do you think?" he asked. "The goal is to achieve a placement that looks like an assembly drawing."

"They look alike," I replied.

"Cut another perforated board of the same dimension like this," he said.

So I went to work with the hacksaw and measuring tape; I cut the piece, filed the edges down, and showed it to Tim.

"Put the blank board away," he said, "continue to study the placement we did this afternoon."

"What is the tiny marking at the end of every chip?" I inquired.

"It is the first pin of the chip. The numbering goes down the left side and wraps around to the opposite side," he said. "The last pin is the one directly opposite the marking."

"Why do you have a one-inch space from the edge of the board to every chip?" I inquired again.

"We need the space to hold the board when we start to work on it," he said. "I consider one inch to be wide enough."

Meanwhile, Spectrametrics had hired three chemists, who walked around in white robes and gloves. They had their own lab connected to the room with the danger sign on the door.

One day, Mr. Keagan came to the lab with a huge man wearing a white robe. And said, "Jimmy, meet Dr. Douglas Michaels. He is a professor at a university in North Dakota, and he is working on the atomic emission spectrometer. Doug, this is Jimmy Olsen. He is designing the computer for the spectrometer. Tim is his partner, and Chuks and Russ are supporting Jimmy."

They exchanged pleasantries and left the lab, then the big guy went back to his lab.

"That guy is huge," Jimmy, joked.

"What would you do," Tim asked, "if you met him in a dark alley?"

"Runaway as fast as I could," Jimmy replied.

On Saturday, very early in the morning, I heard the loud siren of a fire truck blaring outside. I looked outside my window and saw a large crowd in front of my apartment building. Then I saw smoke entering my apartment from the hallway.

Therefore, I put my clothes on in a hurry, threw two trunks in which I saved valuable personal belongings out the window, and then I jumped down from the second floor into the trash bin. I got out of the tray with minor bruises and moved my trunks to Rex and Shegu's apartment. Then we watched the fire consume the entire building from the second floor to the third floor; I lost all my clothes, books, TV, and my radio too.

After the fire, the Red Cross representatives collected the names of the occupants of the building and told us where to go for help. From that day, I stayed with Rex and Shegu and then on Monday, I reported to the office of the dean of international students and explained my situation. Then his office applied for a work permit on my behalf. A few weeks later, I got a work permit from the immigration office before going to the Red Cross office, where they were processing the fire victims.

When I reported for processing, a lady asked, "do you have a police report?"

"Yes, I do," I replied.

Then she gave me a check for two-thousand-five-hundred dollars.

"This check will help you in a small way to find another apartment," the lady said.

I witnessed the Red Cross in action during the Nigeria-Biafra war and saw first hand the fantastic work they did, which was still fresh in my mind. It is fair to say that a greater sense of empathy ought to be had for people who cannot help themselves. After all, I had a work permit by the immigration department, and I was staying with my friends. In my opinion, I was in better condition than others. So I rejected the check and stayed with Rex and Shegu until I moved to my own apartment on South Huntington Avenue.

Throughout that period, I continued to go to work and learned how to wire a computer board—a process called breadboarding. After my final examination, I had a meeting with Mr. Keagan in which he

A MATTER OF FAITH

reminded me that he'd adjust my salary and said, "See me after your graduation."

I remember Russ and I left the office on Friday and stopped to chat in the hallway about the cable we were tripping over in the hallway.

"Doug is generating radiofrequency. That is causing the computers to malfunction when he is working in his lab," I said. "And running cable on the rug along the hallway is not right either."

"You can't say that, because you don't know what he is doing in there," Russ said.

"You are right. Still, I don't think Doug is doing the right thing by running the cable on the rug—along the hallway.

I graduated from Northeastern University on June 15, 1980. And started work the following Monday. I also remembered that Mr. Keagan had told me to see him after my graduation. However, I was uncomfortable discussing my salary; I hate talking about how much I am worth.

However, to my utmost discomfort, Mr. Keagan came to the lab in the afternoon—after lunch and invited me to his office.

"What is the highest salary students in your class got?" he asked.

"I don't know, sir," I replied.

"Well, I know, and I will pay you the same," he said.

"Thank you, sir," I said.

"Don't you care to know how much?" he asked.

"No, sir," I answered.

"OK, you will see it on your next paycheck," he said.

Chapter 5
Welcome To High Tech

There are no jaded, bored people in the high-tech industry, in the land of really good hardcore geeks. They all have a kind of intensity about what they're doing that makes it impossible for them to be bored or passionless. They are pretty driven, and they get a lot of joy from what they do, and it comes through.

~ Neal Stephenson

On Friday, Mr. Keagan invited me to his office again to discuss my criticisms of Doug's work—running a cable along the hallway on top of a rug. "I heard your comments on Doug's work," he said. "Tell me why you think he is not doing the right thing."

"Although I'm not quite sure," I said, "however, running a wire down the hallway on top of the rug as a grounding scheme seems a bit peculiar."

Doug had a PhD in electrical engineering and recommended to work on the company's atomic plasma emission Spectrometer by the president of PlasmaTherm—a company in Pennsylvania and the manufacturer of the system's power supply. He had been at it for six months, and he had not made any progress. Moreover, whatever Doug was doing in the lab, the effect in the engineering lab was creating radio frequency interference, which caused the computers in the lab to malfunction.

When I arrived at work on Monday, a rumor was just breaking that Doug had been fired. For a moment, I thought that I was the cause and felt terrible. Then after lunch, a memo came out and not only confirmed Doug's departure but whipped up my sense of guilt as well.

A MATTER OF FAITH

Regardless, the first time I saw what Doug was working on, I had just entered the lab with Mr. Keagan. He walked around the system and said to me:

"This is the atomic plasma emission power supply," he said. I want you to take over the project and do the best you can; in case you run into any problem don't be afraid to ask me for assistance."

The following day after lunch, another memo came out that I was taking over the development of the atomic plasma emission power supply. Then Russ said, "Chuks, I think Mr. Keagan heard what you said the other day,"

"It's odd for a new college graduate to take on such a project," Tim said. "I am glad that you've finished wiring your board, so I can spare you for the time being."

To begin with, I went to Northeastern University to research atomic plasma emission, but everything I read about it confused me the more rather than help me to get going. Then I checked the company's library; still, I did not find anything relevant to radio frequency interference.

In short, nothing I read about the project during the whole week, gave me any clue as to figuring out what to do or how to start. Then came my self-condemnation for criticizing Doug's work.

Despite my difficulty in getting started, I removed the wire Doug had run along the hallway on the rug and stripped off all the cables connected to the system, including the sign on the door because I did not see the need for it.

The first week ended with me still clueless about how to start. As a result, I began to have a funny feeling and a touch of nervousness. But the fear of failure whipped up my resolve and determination.

On Monday, I began to clean the room and open every piece of paper in it, just to keep busy and give my brain time to boot up. Just as I was dusting off the system, I found a plastic wrap taped to the chimney on top of the system: the atomic plasma emission product specification.

Mildly stated, this specification gave me a clue on how to start. "The system tends to be noisy," the document specified. "It is to be deployed in a quiet room."

Consequently, I became preoccupied with the term *quiet room*, so I searched for the meaning. Most of the interpretations centered on the suppression of noise in the room, nothing electrical. It was all about echo, wall type, ceiling type, and floor type. So I gave up searching.

Suddenly I remembered the steps I had taken back at the Nigerian petroleum refinery to shield the control system from noise and thought, "It has to be the same technique."

Judging from the way things were going, I realized that the project would require time and dedication, so I paid the lady who was babysitting my daughters, Ere and Ugo, for additional four hours so I could work late.

First, I wrote a project plan and gave it to Mr. Keagan. Second, I went on a scan of the *Yellow Pages* in search of the parts I needed for the project. Third, I found the parts and bought them.

After reading the project plan, Mr. Keagan came to the lab for a short meeting we spent talking about the job Doug had done without a plan. Sure, any reasonable person would have accepted Mr. Keagan's approval of my project plan as a compliment. But I did not; instead, I felt a sense of guilt for doing what Doug did not do, again I nervously said, "Sir, I wrote the plan so you won't worry yourself to sick about me screwing everything up."

"It looks like a plan," he said. "I am not worried about you. After all, you've done more than Doug did in six months."

I went to work on Saturday and began to measure the distance between the shallow lake behind the building and the outside wall where the system was deployed, Mr. Keagan arrived and came over.

"How is it going, Chuks?" He inquired.

"I'm about to establish a grounding point for the system," I answered.

"You haven't told me how and where you will get those things you need for the job and how much they will cost," he said.

"I've bought the things I need already."

"What did you buy?" he asked.

A MATTER OF FAITH

"I bought four feet of a copper rod; a hundred-foot roll of three-inch-wide copper strip, a soldering iron, flux, and a roll of solder."

"Do you have the receipt?"

"Yes, sir, it is in the room."

"Put the receipt on my desk," he said. "Anytime you buy anything, including lunch and dinner, during nonworking hours, I want you to give me the receipt."

I terminated the copper strip on the copper rod, drove it into the ground at the waterside, and dug up a trench from the waterside to the building. Next, I threaded the strap through the pipe I had buried in the channel.

Finally, I threaded the strap into the room and bolted the piece to the base of the system.

After visual inspections and testing with instruments, I discovered that most of the metallic parts and electrical connections were seating on the paint, thereby making partial or no metallic contact with each other.

Evidently, that was the pivotal moment when I said to myself, "I have found the problem" so all I had left was the solution.

Therefore, I had at it; I disconnected the parts, scraped the paint off, and restored the electrical connections and felt a bit confident that I was on the right track. After that, the rest was two months of fun.

It had been a while now since anybody turned the system on, and nobody remembered the frustration of watching computers whine and freeze up when Doug turned the system on.

Still, the visual image of employees watching their computers crash haunted me so much that I feared turning the system on despite my confidence in the job I did.

On Friday, Tim asked Russ to come to work on Saturday and help him, so I came to work as well. While Tim was working on his computer, I summoned enough courage and turned the atomic plasma emission power supply on to see what would happen.

Surprisingly, neither Tim nor those who were working on their computers screamed.

Then I became awareness that I was close to succeeding where Doug had failed. However, I recognized my limitations, the yet-to-get-off-the-ground state of my professional life, and suppressed the urge to celebrate or show any emotions. Instead, I sat next to Tim in the lab and assisted him until closing time.

The following week, just out of curiosity, I drew a circle around the system and divided it into six equal sections of sixty degrees.

Of course, I was trying to verify what I read once—that radio-frequency interference radiates in an isotropic pattern.

Therefore, one day, when the office had closed, and the workers had gone home, I began to rotate the system in sixty-degree increments through three-hundred and sixty degrees. At each sixty-degree point, I turned the system off and on, and the computers worked without interference. Then I disconnected the copper strip, separated the joints with plastic sheets, and repeated the exercise. Each time I turned the system off and on, the computers crashed—after whining just as they did when Doug was working on the system providing empirical evidence to the correctness of the job I did.

Then I removed the plastic sheets, reconnected the parts and the copper strip to the system, and spent another month writing the project report. It was my first, so I simply described everything I did step by step before I began the project, the initial actions I took, and everything I did subsequently.

Finally, I showed Mr. Keagan how the system was working, and I gave him the project report. After reading it, he made some changes.

When the executive staff met the following Monday, they discussed the project report and invited me to the meeting.

"Could you give us a quick demo of what you've written in this report?" Mr. Keagan asked. "And what you referred to as isotropic radiation."

So I opened the lab and excused myself to visit the men's room as the staff gathered around the system. You could have guessed it, I was nervous.

Now with all the computers turned on, and employees are working on their own computers as usual. I demonstrated what I had written in the report, and none of the machines whined.

A MATTER OF FAITH

After the demonstration, Mr. Keagan sent a copy to Mr. Nelson Block, the president of PlasmaTherm, and the manufacturer of the atomic plasma emission power supply. A few weeks later, Mr. Keagan received a letter from Mr. Nelson Block and invited me to his office to read it. In that letter, Mr. Nelson ripped my report apart and described it as "total nonsense."

"I will invite Mr. Block over with his chief scientific officer, and we will have you do a demonstration for us in our conference room," he said. "What do you think about that?"

"That will be fine."

"Is three weeks enough time to get the conference room ready?"

"Yes, I believe so, sir," I replied.

As the day of the demonstration got closer, I got nervous. I suspected all the eyes watching me would sicken me. I had a haircut and had my black suit dry-cleaned. Then I sought advice from Jimmy. He told me a story about his first public speech and how his throat dried up and his voice faded and all he could do was cough.

"You have done the work already," he said. "Follow your project report page by page. I read it, and I can tell you it is pretty good. Keep a cup of water or tea by your side."

Before the day of the demonstration, we received one system from PlasmaTherm, which Russ and I moved to the conference room and let it sit in one corner of the room.

On the day of the demonstration, the guests arrived as I was helping Tim to debug my breadboard. While Mr. Keagan was showing them around, he introduced them to Jimmy. Then at nine o'clock, Jimmy joined them in an initial one-hour meeting before I was invited to the conference room.

"This is my new engineer, who took over the system development from Douglas," Mr. Keagan said. "His name is Chuks I. Ndukwe, he graduated from Northeastern University six months ago, and now I will let him show us what he did with the system."

After Mr. Keagan's introduction, I stood up, walked to the system nervously, and began, "I will go through the project report page by page, and I hope everybody has a copy," I said.

I looked around and saw everybody had a copy. So I went from page to page and described what I had done and why. When I got to the final test, I asked the people at the computer stand to report any computer malfunction during the demonstration. Then I turned the system on—and there were no complaints.

I turned to the page where I had described the radio frequency radiated by the system as isotropic. Then I showed them the mapping on the floor. Next, I rotated the system through three-hundred and sixty degrees in sixty-degree increments. At every point, I turned the system off, waited for one minute, and then I turned it on again, and the system behaved the same and nobody complained.

"This concludes part one of the demonstration," I said.

"Let's take a break. We will continue after lunch," Mr. Keagan said.

During lunch, I moved the system to the corner and replaced it with the system we had just received from PlasmaTherm. Then after lunch, I went back to the conference room and continued part two of the demonstration.

"This system was shipped to us from the manufacturer, and nothing has been done to it yet," I said.

I turned the system on, and all the computers whined and crashed.

"If you go back and open chapter two of my project report under the heading 'Initial Tests and Observations,' this is what I was describing."

Then I proceeded to rotate the system in the same manner that I did the first system.

"In effect, what I did was to shield or suppress the radiation from the system. This is the end. Thank you," I concluded.

"Does anybody have any questions for Mr. Chuks?" Mr. Keagan asked.

"Yes, how long did it take you to complete this project?" Jimmy asked.

"It took four months," I answered.

"Thank you, Mr. Chuks. You can go back to the lab," Mr. Keagan said.

I went back to the lab, feeling really warm and fuzzy.

A MATTER OF FAITH

"Did you screw up?" Tim asked.

"No, you wouldn't believe the looks on those people's faces," I said.

"I must say you knocked it out of the ballpark," Tim said.

"What does that mean, Tim?" I inquired.

"Relax, you did well," he said.

After the guests' visit, Mr. Gross, Plasma Therm's chief scientific officer, invited my wife and me to visit them at their office in Mount Lauren, NJ and speak with his development staff.

For reasons described in Mr. Nelson's letter, I did not want to visit Plasma-Therm. However, Mr. Keagan persuaded me to go—noting that the invitation was a form of apology. So my wife and I visited PlasmaTherm and spent a week there.

At the end of the year, PerkinElmer—a company located in California, if I am not mistaken—bought Spectrametrics, so they laid me off. And then I went back to school to continue my studies in computer sciences.

Chapter 6
How Caller ID Began

The secret to getting ahead is getting started.

~ Mark Twain

I had gone back to school mainly to concentrate on computer science because of my passion for programming, order, and logic. For the most part, coding a concept, compiling, and running the program with the wrong result due to improper initialization of the variables reminds me of life.

Similarly, I wonder how perfect Nature's initial conditions must be at the creation of the universe for everything to work in harmony.

Now I am back to school and work a part-time job at Codex Corporation in Stoughton, Massachusetts. The company manufactured modems used to interconnect computers before the commercialization of the Internet. There were a few fresh college graduates and engineers from Northeastern University, Lowell University, MIT, the University of Massachusetts, and so on in my department.

My assignment was to write a program for the recognition of the Bundespost (the German telephone and telegraph regulatory agency) ring signal. I shared a cubicle with an electrical engineer, Larry J. He worked on hardware—things like PCB, ICs, chips, and sockets, and I wrote software programs.

Every country has PTT (postal, telephone, and telegraph) regulations, which each telecommunication product must comply with before the manufacturer sells it in that country. A few weeks earlier, Codex had sent modems to the UK to be tested for agency approval, and so the management was expecting the result.

One summer morning, as Codex employees having breakfast, got the news that "Codex's modem had failed a PTT test in the United

A MATTER OF FAITH

Kingdom." The news brought a chill to the cafeteria and turned lively conversations to absolute silence.

For me, though, I was new and had no idea as to what was going on. Shortly, the engineering manager, Mr. John M., called an emergency meeting. So we gathered in the conference room, and as expected, he made the rumor about the failure of the company's modem official.

"Our modem failed agency test in the United Kingdom this morning," he said. "But we still have three hours to make changes and get it to pass."

"What parameter did it fail?" Peter asked.

"The ring detector came on too fast," John, answered. "I want all of you to come up with a solution before you leave this conference room." Then he locked us in and left.

Immediately, the scramble for a solution began. Some engineers offered equations and ideas, some of which were impractical and others that would take days, if not weeks, to implement.

As I listened to the hardware engineers argue their ideas with each other, I questioned how well they had thought about those ideas. However, the problem was very much a hardware issue, and since I was a software engineer, I did not believe it was my problem.

However, I realized that whoever came up with the solution would be revered in the department, if not in the company as a whole. Still, I was an F1 student and worked part-time, and for that reason, my interest in the whole saga was minimal at best.

When the hardware engineers failed to reach a consensus, the meeting adjourned. So then, I borrowed the modem drawing and the UK ring-detector requirement from Larry and studied them for about thirty minutes. Then I picked a resistor and a capacitor the value of which I determined by calculating their time constant—rise time. So I attached that resistor and capacitor—a simple scheme, to the ring detector circuitry. And after evaluating this model scheme in the lab, the modem passed the ring-detector test.

Then the manager called the United Kingdom and told the Codex representative what to do. In less than two hours, the news came back

~ 55 ~

that the modem had passed the test. So my name spread like wildfire. Shortly, the director of engineering came to my cubicle and congratulated me for my work on the modem. "We've been trying to get our modems approved in the UK for some time," he said. "It's quite ironic that a computer science student would solve such a hardware problem."

To be candid, I believe that it was this simple scheme—a resistor and a capacitor—that launched my professional career in the United States.

> **It was as though I was taking a break from my passion—software design to solve the hardware problem that shone a spotlight on my versatility in electrical engineering.**

The following Monday morning, the manager, John, talked about an AT&T telephone interface in a meeting and how they used a coil in the interface to loop back direct current to the central office.

"We'd like to reduce the size of the modem," he said. "But it is impossible as long as we continue to use the coil. I want a volunteer to look into ways of replacing the coil with something smaller. Our customers don't like the size of our modems."

At the next weekly meeting, he stressed the importance and urgency of reducing the modem size again.

Because he kept looking at me each time he brought up the modem issue, I felt the urge to take on the project. On the one hand, I wanted to work on the project, and the pressure to not volunteer on the other. Then at the end, I said, "I'd like to try, but I don't have enough time to devote to the project." Then he said, "See me after the meeting."

Before I went to see John, the director, invited me to his office. Then he advised me to pursue my graduate studies on a part-time basis. "That way, you will maintain your front-running seniority in the business and also continue your masters, which your employer will pay for."

Then after my meeting with Mr. Olsen, I met with John in his office and similarly, the meeting went something like this:

A MATTER OF FAITH

"Chuks, I want to let you know that I am prepared to offer you a full-time position and pay your tuition fees if you take on the project."

✷ ✷ ✷

With his assurance in mind, I changed my student status from full time to part-time and began to work on the project of modifying the AT&T telephone interface.

When I came up with a schematic diagram of what I thought the new interface would be, I showed it to John, expecting compliments; instead, he said, "The general concept looks OK, but the part you selected does not seem right. so find a better part that will do the same job."

One day in the lab, I tried one of the parts—a field-effect transistor, or FET, I had selected, but it went up in flames, and everybody cheered as the smoke rose to the ceiling. Next, I tried a power transistor a week later, and it too overheated and blew up.

Obviously, those initial failures testified to my lack of understanding of the characteristics of the parts I had selected, not necessarily any flaws in the concept of the design.

On one occasion, when I bumped into John in the hallway on his way back from the cafeteria, he asked how my project was going.

"I've fused up the two transistors I selected, and I'm searching for a different type," I said. And then John gave me a catalogue of transistors.

"Look through the section captioned Darlington Array Transistors," he advised.

With the catalogue in hand, I spent hours every day studying the different configurations of the Darlington array transistors, and their characteristics. Then I made my selection after learning their limitations. Then I tried one of the settings, and this time, it worked without blowing up. Now spurred on by the latest result, I tried different combinations until I found a set that worked in compliant to the current requirements and demonstrated it to John.

"We are not there yet," he said. "We have to replace the transformer to reduce the interface to the desired size."

Chuks I, Ndukwe

At first, I felt clueless as to where I'd find a miniature transformer. And then I looked through catalogues and publications until I gave up. I realized the obvious—that the project was not at all trivial. Obviously if it were, somebody could have knocked it off earlier, so I kept going.

One day, John came to my cubicle with a guest, Mr. Siegel, who represented a company in the UK that specialized in miniature transformers so, during our brief conversation; he said, "They could make a custom transformer for me if I gave him the specifications."

Feeling a sense of relief, I gave him the specifications before he left. Then a few weeks later, the receiving clerk gave me a package from the United Kingdom containing the specifications of the transformers the company was working on. After reviewing the specs, John called the company up and asked, "What's the lead time?"

"Four weeks," they said.

"OK, you can proceed," John, said.

Now feeling in the same way as a runner close to crossing the finish line, I put forward two design proposals: one for a generic telephone interface and another for direct-access arrangement, or DAA.

Immediately John called a review meeting, during which the management approved both proposals. Then I began the design while waiting for the transformer. Two months later, the receiving clerk delivered the transformer to me.

So I put the project in full motion; I finished the design, built it, and had a short meeting with John to review the interface. Then he said, "Chuks hand over the interface to Keith LaMotte for testing, and continue with your software design."

At first, I felt offended by his decision thinking John should have allowed me to test the finished product before handing it over to Keith. Then I realized that I still had to complete my software project and so I handed the telephone-interface card to Keith and withheld the DAA card. A few months later, at the weekly meeting, John announced that he had submitted a new modem with the slim-profile interface card and my ring-signal-detection software in it for approval in Germany, which was one of the strictest countries in which to get modem approval.

On the Friday of the approval test, we waited for news from Germany until lunchtime. Then we began to accept the possibility that

A MATTER OF FAITH

the approval test did not go well—despite the difference in the time zone. For me the old saying "No news is good news" still holds true.

Suddenly, just as employees were coming back from lunch, the news came: 'Codex's modem passed German product approval test." Immediately, the company began to buzz with jubilation.

Meanwhile, my officemate, Keith, was still at lunch. So I waited for him by the receptionist's desk while employees were coming back from lunch.

"What's going on?" Larry asked the receptionist as he entered the lobby.

"We got approved in Germany," she said.

Keith—the engineer I handed the telephone interface to for final test, Larry, and I joined the celebration in the conference room.

"You did it," they said.

Finally, the director of engineering, Mr. Olsen, closed the celebration with an optimistic view of the future and congratulatory remarks. "Today's result," he said, "is the reason we invest in young people."

I remember that evening, while I was having dinner with my family the phone rang.

"Hello, who is calling?" my daughter Ugo asked. "Daddy, it is for you."

"Hello, this is Chuks," I answered.

"This is Attorney Silverson. I want to let you know that I have filed an appeal with the immigration review board in Washington, DC, to overturn your case," he said. "I think we have a good chance of succeeding. Keep your fingers crossed."

Earlier in 1980, I had filed for a green card just after my graduation from college, but after several hearings, the Immigration and Naturalization Services denied my application. So I appealed their decision immediately.

The next morning, as I was entering the Codex's office building the receptionist, Mrs. Ester Forbes, stopped me and said, "Mr. Ervin Forbes wants to see you."

"Who is Ervin Forbes?" I asked.

"My husband," she said. "He is a manager at Microcom in Norwood."

"Why does he want to see me?"

"I am not sure."

"When does he want me to see him?"

"You can go tomorrow during lunch," she said. "Ervin's office is right there on Route One."

The following day, I met Mr. Forbes in his office at Microcom for a short meeting we spent discussing the news of Codex's modem approvals in Europe.

"Yes, Ester told me about you. How are you?" Mr. Forbes inquired.

"I am fine, thank you," I replied.

"We have been trying to get our modems approved in the United Kingdom, Germany, and Australia without success," he said. "And I believe that you can help us like you helped Codex."

I realized that he wanted me to join his company, also I recognized the risk of making such a move at a time when my visa was out of status. So I explained my situation regarding job mobility to him.

"Can you stop by on your way home from work? I will be waiting for you," he said.

So on my way home, I stopped at Microcom again to see Mr. Forbes.

"What do you think we can do to get approval in Europe?" he asked.

"Do you have European PTT regulations?" I asked.

"No, how can we get them?"

"Your salespeople can get them," I replied.

Intending to yank a suggestion out of me, Mr. Forbes gave me the modem he had on his desk and the schematic, and then he asked me whether it was good enough for approval in any European country. But I refused to offer any suggestion; instead, I explained the difficulty of trying to get a domestic product approved in Europe.

"This is the deal," he said. "If you join Microcom, we will work with your attorney and file an immigrant-visa application on your behalf, besides, we will pay you more money than you are getting at

Codex." Then he invited his boss, Mr. Charles Sauka, the director, to talk to me.

"Hello, Mr. Chuks. We heard that you got Codex on the roll," he said. "We don't want to play around; we want you at Microcom. Has Ervin told you what we are willing to do for you if you decide to join us?"

"I have to talk with my attorney about that," I said.

When I went home that evening, I called attorney Silverson and told him what Mr. Forbes had told me.

"It sounds like a wonderful idea," he said. "Do you understand the kind of visa they are talking about?"

"No, I don't."

"It's the kind of visa reserved for foreigners who are coming to this country with exceptional technical ability," he said. "It means that the company is having difficulty finding Americans to do the job they want you to do for them. Give my number to Mr. Forbes and have him call me."

One day, I got a phone call from attorney Silverson, and It went something like this:

"Mr. Ndukwe, I talked to Mr. Forbes and Mr. Sauka regarding their offer to get you over to their company, we are moving ahead with the filing of your immigrant visa. We will do that and wait for the outcome of the appeal on your original case. So feel free to join them."

The following day, I went to see Mr. Forbes during my lunch break to seal the deal.

"How much are you making?" he asked.

Given that I always felt reluctant to discuss money during interviews, I handed my last pay stub to him. "I will be right back," he said. He made a copy of it and gave the original back to me. Then he conferred with Mr. Sauka and told me they had decided to pay me twenty-five percent more than what Codex was paying me.

"OK, when do you want me to start?" I asked.

"You can start as soon as you can."

"I will start two weeks from Monday," I said.

"Stop by on your way home from work, and fill out the necessary forms," he advised, and I left.

When I submitted my two weeks' notice on Friday, John said, "Everybody thinks that you have a great future here at Codex, why are you jeopardizing it?"

"I am joining a company that is willing to file an immigrant visa application on my behalf."

"OK, good luck," he replied.

Two weeks later, on July 1987, I reported at Microcom in the next town over from Roslindale, where I lived and met with Mr. Peterson, the human resources manager, and then my manager. Mr. Forbes introduced me around as an international research-and-development engineer. Also, he dedicated a section of the lab for global products and called it the "*PTT Product Lab.*"

Six months later, I had the first Microcom's international modem featuring my DAA ready for UK approval. At that time, Microcom's European sales representative named Martin lived in Sydney, Australia, and he was the guy who took the modem to the United Kingdom for approval.

One day, Mr. Martin arrived at Microcom one day after the modem approval and announced the news. Then we had a meeting in the conference room while the employees celebrated.

"Chuks, could you explain the design?" Martin said. "I noticed something unique about it while it was being tested."

So I spread the schematic on the table and explained how the modem connects directly to the central telephone office, even in idle mode—when the modem is waiting for a ring signal.

"That's my reason for calling it direct-access arrangement," I explained.

"We are looking at an amazing new modem feature in this design," Martin said. "We can ask the central office to send the name and number of the call originator while the modem is ringing."

A MATTER OF FAITH

He described the design as brilliant and joked that he'd make lots of money selling the feature alone. Then he added; "Chuks Figure out how to get the modem to display the incoming number."

After the meeting, I included Caller-ID in my product description document and explained how the modem could receive data in idle mode. Then I warned that the DSP had to be able to process the data and display it on the screen. So I called this feature *incoming-number identification* feature.

Having achieved the initial goal of getting the Microcom's modem approved in the United Kingdom, I began to design a German modem. And completed it four months later, Then Martin got approval from the Germany Bundespost.

By then, my name was getting around the telecommunications industry as the marketing people from other companies were calling to inquire about my DAA interface.

One evening, at dinner, I got a call from attorney Silverson.

"Chuks, the FBI has concluded your background check, and everything is on the up-and-up," he said. "You should be getting a letter from the INS shortly to travel to Nigeria to have your immigrant visa application processed."

"Couldn't the application be processed here in the United States?" I asked. "If I am denied, I will not be able to come back to the United States."

"I am aware of that," he said. "But there is nothing we can do about that. However, I am optimistic because no single question had been raised by either the FBI or the Immigration and Naturalization Service regarding your status."

In March 1990, I received a letter from the immigration office giving me a date to report to the American embassy in Lagos, Nigeria, with the documents listed in the message.

Therefore on August 7, 1990, I traveled to Nigeria. Then on the day of my appointment, I reported at the embassy with all the necessary papers. The initial interview went very well, as it was confined to my technical expertise.

"What is INI?" the consul asked.

"Incoming-number identification," I answered.

"Do you know of any person or entity working on this technology anywhere else in the world or any publication relating to the technology?" he asked.

"No, I do not know sir."

"How does it work?"

"The modem has direct access to the information on the central telephone office." "It collects the originating telephone number and displays it on the modem's display device while the phone rings."

"Can I use it on my telephone set?" he asked.

"No, sir, unless your phone is equipped with an FSK data processor and a display device," I said.

"I would like you to go to the police headquarters and obtain a no-record certification," the consul said. "See the embassy-approved doctor for a physical examination and vaccinations and come back for the final interview," Then the consul gave me a pamphlet with the listing of the places he mentioned. The following day, I went to the police headquarters at Dodan Barrack and got a no-record certification. Then I went to the doctor, who conducted my physical exam and vaccinations and gave me a sealed envelope for the embassy.

On August 10, 1990, I went back to the embassy for a final interview with the same consul who interviewed me before. On arrival, I handed the two envelopes to him; he went through the contents and put them away without questions. My anxiety level shot up as I stared at the consul's face. Then he opened a file before him and said, "Everybody entering the United States has to be screened for AIDS and VD. Also, they must have a certificate from the police department that the individual is not a criminal, In that regard, you are clean," then he asked, "where did you live when you first arrived in the United States, and where do you live currently?"

"I lived at Eleven College Road in Burlington, Massachusetts. And now I live in my house at Twenty-Five Wilmington Street in Brockton, Massachusetts," I answered.

"On behalf of the president and people of the United States of America, I welcome you to the United States," he said. "Your visa will be issued to you on your arrival at the port of entry. Congratulations."

A MATTER OF FAITH

With a sense of relief, I spent a few days in Ghana with my brother Dick and his family before returning to the United States.

On August 14, 1990, I arrived at JFK International Airport in New York on that blistering summer day very anxious to have my visa issued and call my attorney.

Finally, it happened, and then I rushed to the pay-phone, shoved quarters into the machine and called my attorney.

"Counsel, this is Chuks I. Ndukwe. I am back in the United States. I just arrived at JFK, and I've received my immigrant visa," I said with a sense of relief.

"Guess what?" he asked. "Your appeal of the original case was granted. Now you have two green cards. Isn't that amazing? Welcome home, my friend."

By all appearances, my trip to Nigeria was a huge success. Finally, I arrived at work on Monday, August 20, 1990, with a sense of gratitude, and determined to live up to Microcom's expectations of getting their modems approved in every country in Europe.

But that expectation would not last. In January 1991, the news broke that Microcom had been sold to Multitech—another modem company I had not heard of before.

Consequently, Microcom laid me off. Then one day in winter, February 1991, I received a telephone call from Mr. McCarthy.

"This is the Ndukwe residence," Ugo said. "Who is calling? Daddy, it's for you."

"This is Chuks," I said.

"My name is J. McCarthy, a vice president at USRobotics in Skokie, Illinois," he said. "I would like you to visit so we can chat."

"I would like that," I replied.

"OK, I will send you a round-trip plane ticket by overnight mail," he said. "A limousine driver will meet you at O'Hare International Airport on Friday, and I will see you in my office on Monday."

On Monday, February 11, Miss Gavana, Mr. McCarthy's secretary, greeted me on my arrival at USRobotics. We chatted before she directed me to Mr. McCarthy's large office, around which he had his company's modems displayed.

Mr. McCarthy began the interview by telling me about his company and the international telecom expo underway in Hanover, Germany.

"I came back from Germany just to chat with you," he said. "When I was there, your name came up quite a bit. Is it true that you got modems approved for Codex and Microcom in the United Kingdom and Germany?"

"That's true, sir," I said.

"How long did you work for Codex?"

"Three years."

"How long were you at Microcom?"

"Three years as well."

"How much are you asking?"

"Sir, I don't feel comfortable negotiating my salary," I said. "Make me an offer when I get home."

After returning home, Mr. McCarthy called me and made an offer that was much more than I had anticipated. I also recognized that I was unemployed, so I accepted his offer.

"When are you starting?" he asked. "I need you here ASAP."

"I'd like to start on Monday, February 18," I said.

"All right, I'll have a moving company arrange for your relocation," he said. "See you then."

The moving company arrived in Brockton on February 16 and loaded my belongings in the truck, including my car. Then I left Brockton on February 17 and arrived in Chicago in the evening.

Chapter 7
Following The Guide

...when you put your life in a good place, good things follow.

~ Willie Nelson

When I arrived at USRobotics in Skokie, Illinois, on February 18, 1991, the company had arranged for me to stay in a private home—bed and breakfast, in Evanston, Illinois, until I found an apartment. So the company hired a real-estate management company to help find a suitable apartment for me to rent or a house to buy—whichever I chose.

On my first day at work, Mr. McCarthy dropped off two modems in my office—a Courier and a Sportster. Then he told me to review the two modems and determine why they were failing approvals in Europe.

The first thing I noticed when I opened the Courier modem was the zinc-coated cardboard covering the Telephone-interface section of the modem. This was a clear indication that the engineers who developed the modem did not understand the basic concept of electrical shielding.

The next thing I noticed was that the engineers had changed a few domestic-modem parts to achieve specific test results. Additionally, I flagged a few other safety issues and reported my observations to Mr. McCarthy the following day. And noted: "The current design is seriously flawed in its implementation, by all accounts, it is a domestic modem."

"Is there anything we can do to get it to comply with international requirements?" he asked.

"They do not meet international safety requirements and operational specifications," I said. "It will be hard to get then approved in Europe as they are."

In any event, I did not intend to demean the efforts of the design engineers by my comments. On the contrary, I believed that they did their best based on their knowledge and experience.

The following day, Mr. McCarthy gave me a plane ticket and a credit card, and went back to Germany tonight. Then he said, "I will pick you up at Frankfurt airport in Germany on Sunday."

Before departing for Germany, I rented an apartment at one hundred sixty-nine Ridge Avenue in Chicago. Then I gave Miss Gavana, the key to the apartment so the maintenance people could move my belongings in should the moving truck arrive in my absence.

On Sunday, March three, I arrived at Frankfurt airport at ten o'clock in the morning. And then Mr. McCarthy picked me up and drove straight to the CeBIT—the International Telecommunication Exposition in Hanover, where the crew greeted us at the USRobotics booth. After introducing me to the team, he showed me around the expo and returned to the United States.

The expo was a magnificent display of engineering wonders. The whole world was there as every country showed off its best in telecommunication engineering.

I remember walking around all day to visit the booths of the famous American companies until my feet began to ache; that was how large it was.

Despite my aching feet, I visited all the postal, telephone, and telegraph (PTT) booths. I signed my name in their visitor logbooks and requested copies of their rules and regulations. Also, I visited most, if not all, of the modem manufacturers' booths and played with their modems. Then I took copies of their product specifications.

I returned to the United States on Sunday, March seventeen, and compiled my trip report after recovering from jet lag and gave it to Mr. McCarthy to his utter surprise. The report included my views about USRobotics' competitors' modems, the traffic in those companies' booths compared to that of USRobotics' and my conversation with the German students.

A MATTER OF FAITH

The students had expressed their views about USRobotics' modems, which they loved and nicknamed Black Machine.

Expectedly, the moving company had delivered my belongings while I was in Germany. So I spent time sorting them out and went to work late on Monday. Surprisingly, the receptionist, Miss Howard, and a few other employees coming out of the cafeteria greeted me with "congratulations." "What could that be for?" I wondered.

Then I logged into my computer and discovered that Mr. McCarthy had sent out a memo announcing my promotion to manager of the international research and development department.

Still, I had not met the person I took over the department from, but I heard that he traveled to Sweden but never came back to his office.

Honestly, I felt awkward managing the department after I had criticized the work they did for years. I also felt guilty of taking over the management of the department from their friend.

Still, I realized USRobotics hired me to do the job right and shut those emotions off. But as could be expected, my promotion was not well received.

I began my first-week meeting the engineers face-to-face, on a one-on-one basis, to sell my ideas, and explain my expectations for the job the company expected us to do.

During my first weekly meeting, I posted our mission statement on the board and handed a copy to each engineer. Then a few minutes later, Mr. McCarthy joined the meeting and grabbed a copy too. The mission statement read:

> **The International Research and Development Department of USRobotics will strive to be the best in the industry by designing and developing quality products on a timely basis, getting approval in every country, and meeting the company's time-to-market objectives.**

"I stopped by to let all of you know that Mr. Ndukwe has my backing in what he is planning to achieve in this company," Mr.

McCarthy said. "Mr. Ndukwe, I would like to see you in my office after your meeting." And then he left.

The short meeting was spent discussing how it feels when a modem fails approval testing and the exhilaration when it passes. I tried to get my engineers out of the progressive tiredness and malaise, a loss of pep, and inability to work effectively. I told them how I felt the first time my design passed approval tests in the United Kingdom and Germany and my anguish waiting for the result of the tests. I believe it was that story that changed their minds about me. They had not heard from somebody—in person who got modems approved in the United Kingdom and Germany before. Indeed, it was a pep talk I never imagined its impact.

"If you agree with the mission statement, please sign your copy, and return it to me before the end of the day," I said and concluded the meeting. Then I met with Mr. McCarthy in his office one hour before lunch.

"How are you feeling?" he asked. "I was blown away when I read your mission statement; it is brilliant."

"Thank you, sir," I said.

"I just want to warn you," he said. "The people you are working with do not have reputations as productive engineers in this establishment."

"I sensed it on my arrival."

"How did you know that?"

"When you asked me to review the international products," I said. "The first thing I noticed was that the engineers were merely changing the values of a few parts of the domestic modem without a basic understanding of the international product specifications."

"Let's go to lunch," he said.

Then we went to Mama Leona, an Italian joint renowned for its lasagna, and spent two hours going over my trip report, especially my observations about a portfolio of pocket-size and palm-top modems made by another company, *Worldport*.

"I'm in negotiations to acquire that company," John said. After lunch, he gave me a check for five thousand dollars on our way back to the office. "This ought to last till you get paid in two weeks," he said.

A MATTER OF FAITH

For one thing, It was a perfect time for a man who'd handed over his bank account to his estranged wife before arriving in Chicago. So I opened a bank account with that check.

Then at my next weekly meeting, I distributed the project schedules and approvals for the United Kingdom, Germany, France, and Australia. And then I invited each person to choose the project he or she wanted to work on.

For the most part, it was letting my engineers choose their projects instead of forcing projects on them, that unleashed their potential and dedication to their projects. They owned their projects and left me free only to guide and provide algorithms when necessary.

At the next meeting, I gave them copies of the country-specific-design-specifications I had written based on each country's PTT regulations.

Within a few weeks, my engineers transformed the boring lab into a lively workshop; I had to lock the lab to force them to go home at the end of the day.

One day, John stopped by my office to chat and said, "I stopped by your lab, and I couldn't believe how active your people are, how is the new design going?"

"We are conducting final lab tests," I said. "I will take the modems to the field test site in Aurora next week for emission and safety tests, and then I will release them officially for PTT approval."

The following week, I went to Aurora and had the modems tested. While I was there, I made minor tweaks to get the modems to pass the test and then I released them for approval tests in the United Kingdom and Germany.

On Monday morning, John came to my office with a gentleman who had a smile on his face when they walked into my office.

"Chuks, I want you to meet a friend of mine," John said. "He is our managing director for the European sales division and his name is Martin Franklin."

Like friends who had found each other after a long separation, Martin spread his hands, and he and I embraced each other.

"How are you, Chuks? Good to see you," he said.

"It's so good to see you, Martin," I echoed.

When we sat down for a brief meeting, Martin brought up the issue we first discussed at Microcom.

"How far have you gone with that INI stuff?" Martin asked. "It's been on my mind since we spoke last at Microcom."

"Chuks, this is the man who told me to go after you when I was in Germany," John said. "And I can tell you he is as happy as I am that you are here."

"I need that INI stuff in the Australian modem," Martin said. "The central office in Sydney is ready to make an allowance for it."

"What is, INI?" John asked.

"That's the feature I told you Chuks was working on at Microcom before they sold the company: incoming number identification," he said. "It allows the modem to receive the incoming number and the name of the call originator from the central telephone office during the ringing period and display the information on the screen for the call receiver to see."

"Are you sure?" John asked.

"Yes, we can sell this feature as a caller ID," Martin said.

In effect, that was the genesis of what is known today as "Caller ID."

"What do you need to complete the implementation of this feature?" John asked. "And how long will it take?"

"My part is done," I said. "We need the DSP department to get involved so they can answer that question." Immediately, John invited the DSP department manager, Mike, to join us, and then I repeated what I said about the feature and what was left to complete its implementation.

"How long will it take to finish it?" John asked again.

"We currently display lots of information on the screen," Mike said. "I would say a matter of weeks or one month in the worst case."

Finally, I told the DSP manager to process the data and display it before the modem transmits the answer tone.

A MATTER OF FAITH

✱ ✱ ✱

After the meeting, I demonstrated the Australian modem performance to Martin and John at the lab, and as usual, Martin responded with "Brilliant," "I will call you when I return from Europe."

On Friday, just as we were leaving the lab for lunch, Martin called from London. And said, "we've got approval in Germany and the United Kingdom." Immediately, John sent out a memo announcing the news that sent the company into a celebratory frenzy. So we cheered and went out to lunch at a pizza shop.

A month later, the DSP department gave me a PROM in which they included the INI feature; I tested it in my lab, and it worked. When Martin called from Australia, we could definitely see his number and his name on the modem screen. Then I tested the feature at the DSP lab again to their delight.

Finally, I called Martin back and informed him that the test was successful. Then I released the modem to John's office to send to Australia for approval. A few weeks later, John sent out a memo that "we've gotten another approval in Australia and the caller ID worked flawlessly," he said, and congratulated my department.

I realized that my engineers had earned the recognition they deserved in the company by getting our modems approved in European countries. Still, we had not done the French modem yet. So everybody joined in on the French project. Now you could see three or four engineers staring at the computer screen, pointing at data points and sometimes laughing. It was how I had hoped they would behave.

On Friday, late in the afternoon, checks had gone out to all employees, but I did not receive mine. Later I got a call from the payroll manager.

"You might be wondering why you didn't get your check," she said. "The IRS has garnished your wages, and I would advise you to seek an attorney's help."

Immediately, I began to flip the *Yellow Pages* until I found an attorney who specialized in tax cases. I went to his office in downtown

Chicago right away, filled out forms, and paid him a retainer fee for a bankruptcy filing. Then I flew to Brockton and advised my estranged wife to direct all legal inquiries to me. And then I returned to Chicago. The following week, I received my paycheck, and a few months later, I went for a hearing. In the end, my bankruptcy filing was approved, and my debt—mortgage payments and taxes on my houses in Brockton—was discharged.

Now, I was helping my brother Dickson get his business on track. So I began ordering used clothing from Germany and redirecting the shipment to Ghana to get him back into active trading.

On October 9, 1991, I boarded a plane and took off for Geneva, Switzerland, and arrived on October 10 to assist USRobotics' crew run the International Telecommunication Exposition there.

At the end of the expo, on October 17, USRobotics representatives held a gala at the hotel ballroom. I was too busy making arrangements for the French modem approval, so I missed most of the occasion.

As I walked into the ballroom, Martin had already accepted an USTelecom91 lapel pin on my behalf and was making his remarks. Then he paused and said, "now, here's the manager of the year, the man who gave the world Caller ID." Then he waved me up to the podium and pinned the lapel on my suit.

As the fiscal year gradually came to an exciting end, Mr. McCarthy invited me to a product planning meeting spent allocating money for my department. I had put together my product development plan for the next fiscal year to dominate the international modem market, which Hayes dominated in the past by Hayes Modem. I projected two modem approvals per quarter in every country where USRobotics did business.

"Isn't that too ambitious?" John asked.

"For me, it's a goal to strive for," I said.

At the end of the meeting, my budget for the next year, including five thousand dollars for my team-building efforts, came to a total of eight-hundred-thousand dollars. Then John reimbursed me two thousand, five hundred dollars I had spent to build my team the previous year.

A MATTER OF FAITH

On November 29, 1992, I traveled again to Ghana to get a better understanding of my brother's business conditions. Then I returned to the United States on December 14.

When I went to work the following Monday, I had to make a tough decision. On the one hand, I was doing very well at my job, but on the other hand, my brother's business was weary, to say the least, and he needed me.

I slid down my mental slope —where I make serious decisions. And I found nobody to talk me out of quitting my job and devoting my time to helping my brother—indeed, nobody to pull the brake on human behavior.

And wholly blinded to the risks of the decision I was about to make, I quit my job and started a used-clothing export business to help my brother. So I sent for him to come to the United States for six months and teach me how to grade the clothes.

Before he left the United States, I filled a warehouse with a forty-foot truckload of used clothes, bought a baling machine, and went into production mode.

When my brother went back to Ghana, I began to ship containers of used clothing to Ghana without getting any money in return. As a result, the business collapsed under its own weight.

So I got evicted from my apartment and the warehouse. However, before I moved out, I got up one night and checked the job-opening-section in the newspaper—*The Sun-Times.* I found an opening for a senior electrical engineer at ADC Telecommunications in Minnetonka, Minnesota so I emailed my résumé to the company. Then the company replied on Monday and invited me for an interview.

When I arrived at Saint Paul International Airport, the weather was a few degrees below zero and ice covered the road. Still, I drove to the hotel in Plymouth, Minnesota, where the company had made a reservation for me to stay. Then it snowed again that night, and the temperature dropped like a rock to twenty-five degrees below zero.

On my way to the company for the interview, the highway was deserted, and driving was treacherous. Nevertheless, I drove carefully in low gear and at a crawl until I arrived at ADC Telecommunications.

There were only two cars in the parking lot, and the company was closed. But surprisingly, the vice president and the hiring manager were in their offices.

During the interview, which was much as a friendly chat as can be imagined, they wanted to know how much money I wanted for salary.

"I would like you to call me when I get home and make me an offer," I said. "I do not like to talk about money during an interview."

After the interview, I drove straight to Saint Paul's airport and boarded a plane back to Chicago and later in the evening, I received a call from ADC.

"Hello, Mr. Chuks, my name is Liz Ryan. I am calling from ADC Telecom in Minnesota. Did you have a good flight back?" she inquired.

"Yes, ma'am, I had a wonderful flight back."

"Have you made up your mind on how much you want for a salary?"

"Let's start with your offer," I said.

Then she called back and made an offer, which I rejected. Then she increased the, which I accepted.

"The president, Mr. Don Sweeney, and Mr. Kamath, your manager, want to know when you'll start," she said.

"I will start on Monday," I replied.

"You can go straight to the same hotel you stayed at when you came here for your interview," she said. "We've arranged for you to stay there till you find an apartment. I will see you on Monday."

Chapter 8
Problem Solver

Every solution to every problem is simple. It's the distance between the two where the mystery lies.

~ Derek Land

One thing about not living with your children or changing jobs is that you change your address too. And then you worry that they'd call your old telephone number and hear, "The number you called is out of service. Check the number and call again." That thought haunted me every time I changed my job—my address and telephone number too. So when I arrived in Minnesota, I drove to Plymouth and checked in at the hotel I'd stay in till I found my apartment, the first thing I did was to call my children in Brockton to inform them—as always.

"Hello, Ugo. I just moved to Minnesota, and I would like you and your sisters to come and see where Daddy will be living," I said.

Now, as if in a tussle, I heard Ugo say at the background "let me speak to Daddy" and then Chika said at the foreground as if she was moving the phone away from Ugo, "Daddy come and get us," At that instant my heart lit up with joy as I visualized the scene. Then my ex cut in. "I am coming with them,"

Still fresh in my mind was the happy memory of their previous visits—watching them walk out of the plane arrival gate—each behind the other. So waking up the following morning, I walked down to the lobby-office of the travel agency, bought plane tickets and sent them to my children and then a week later, they arrived at Saint Paul International Airport as Daddy proudly waited. Then we drove to the hotel to my kids' delight.

"Wow, Daddy, your apartment is beautiful," Ugo, said.

Chuks I, Ndukwe

"Can we live here, Mommy?" Chika inquired jokingly, knowing what the reaction would be. Later, we went out and had dinner at an Italian restaurant. Like a re-creation of life when we were living together, we pulled chairs close together and then we discussed those nagging issues such as schoolwork, homework, and their grades, plus their buggy teachers, some of whom I had met several times before.

Then they took their baths while Daddy went to the hotel lobby and came back with a large bowl of popcorn. After they had changed and gotten comfortable, we watched TV as we scooped handfuls of popcorn without looking at the bowl and threw it all in our mouths until they fell asleep.

I have to say, it was gratifying for me to see those beautiful little angels I'd chase around the house, to pick up pieces of paper they had dropped on the floor and forgot to pick up or yell at to turn off the light and go to sleep.

It was amazing feeling looking at my children—unique gifts my mother told me I'd receive when I doubted I would have children of my own for no other reason than how children loved to mess with me as their favorite toy—in my early years.

Still, I worried about them, concerned about the pain and anguish that lied in wait for all of us and how events we hadn't imagined yet would shortchange their sweet lives.

Yet, I hoped it would not be for the worst. Then I thought of my name, which means, "I believe in God," in the boundless mercy of the creator. Therefore, I took refuge in the comfort of my faith; I kissed them on the forehead and went to bed.

At that time, my friends had been calling me from Boston to inform me that my ex was spreading lies about me trying to kill her before I moved to Chicago—obviously that was the excuse she cooked up for not moving to Chicago with me—instead of telling them the truth.

What truth?

That she had had a baby out of wedlock before joining me in the US and refused to talk to me about it, knowing I would never even swat a fly on her back if it would cause her any pain.

So that night, as I lay in bed quietly, with the TV off—hoping my ex would fall asleep in the living room with the kids, suddenly, the door swung open and then she got in the bed, took her clothes off, and proceeded to take my pajamas off.

Let me ask you this question lest my action comes across as rude. Would you cuddle with a person who wants to kill you? I would not. So I pushed her hands gently away, and sat up and said with a muffled tone: "What the hell are you doing? Despite spreading a rumor about me trying to kill you, and now you are conveniently brushing your lies aside and are on a plane to visit the man you accused of trying to kill you. As if that was not disgusting enough, you jump in bed to make love to him.

First, you are not my wife anymore. Second, you ought to be ashamed of yourself. I'll sleep in this room for only one reason: not to horrify my children." Then I buttoned my pajamas up and lay down.

Besides, I spent one week with my children visiting my office, the Mall of America, and the lakes.

Finally, on their departure day, on our way to the airport, Chika said, "Daddy, it's your turn to come and spend one week with us."

"I will come, sweetheart, when time permits," I replied.

Earlier as we walked to the car before taking off for the airport, I had watched everybody's face and sensed something sinister was going to happen from the look on my ex's face, but I did not know what it would be.

Still getting to the airport, we ate ice cream while waiting for their departure announcement and then when the announcement came over the sound system, I escorted them to the boarding gate, hugged them, stood there, and watched them until they disappeared behind the boarding gate. I must confess it was a joyful week for me, which unfortunately turned out to be the last time I would see my kids for a long time.

✱ ✱ ✱

I had settled into my job; my office was a cubicle, and my title, "senior engineer," quite different from the previous title "manager." I began to learn about the hybrid fiber-coax (HFC) technology and how I'd fit within the larger scheme of things.

ADC's HFC system shared some features with the modem technology, the line interface. Therefore, I took comfort in my familiarity with those shared features. I knew I was as good as anybody in the telecommunication industry.

Mr. Mike Wanless's cubicle was next to mine, and he had joined ADC from Tellabs, another modem company. Mike was strictly a hardware engineer, whereas I had a combination of software and hardware expertise, and more importantly, I had years of management experience he did not have. In many ways, our combined expertise added a certain level of versatility to the department and equipped us with the ease with which we worked closely on issues that required an expert opinion. Mike was so good at testing the HFC line cards, so he focused on that and let me handle software issues.

A few months after I joined the company, they promoted Mr. Kamath, to the position of a director, and Mike to the status of a manager. So after the announcement, I went to Mike's office to congratulate him. Then I asked, "where are we going for lunch to celebrate?"

"Let's go to a Chinese restaurant. I have something to tell you," Mike said.

"I don't eat Chinese food," I replied. "I think I am allergic to it."

"OK, how about a steak house?"

"That sounds good," I said.

When we got to the steak house, he ordered beer, and I ordered Pepsi. Then he began his story.

"Chuks, I don't want to be a manager," he said. "I wish Uma had talked to me before making the announcement. You've been a manager for years, so you should take the job."

"Are you drunk? don't be silly, Mike," I said. "You can't pass up an opportunity like that. Look, I will help you in any way you want. Take the job and pretend that you love it. I will help prepare your briefing for Monday staff meetings. Hang in there after two to three times, you will become comfortable."

"Did you feel nervous when you became a manager?" he asked.

A MATTER OF FAITH

"No, my circumstance was different. I had all the encouragement and appreciation I needed before I was promoted to the position," I said. "The vice president of the company had the confidence that I could do the job, and the company needed my expertise as well."

"I have been working here for four years," he said, "and things haven't been rosy in the department. That's why I am worried."

"Don't worry. Everything will work out fine," I reassured Mike.

I believe it was that chat at the restaurant that brought us together as the friends we became later. Every day after work, we spent one hour together going over existing technical issues, some of which I'd volunteer to work on, such as the malfunctioning of the HFC system.

For reasons unknown at the time, the test department was conducting final tests, but the system would not work correctly. The software department claimed that the system worked flawlessly in their lab. On the flip side, Mike had done thorough testing with central-office switchgear and did not see any problem either. So at a staff meeting, Mike proposed the formation of a team of three engineers to evaluate the problem and nominated me to lead the team. The executive staff agreed, and then they asked me to lead the team.

When we started, there was no data to review, and no test explicitly dedicated to evaluating the system data flow. But we gleaned from watching the test engineers as they conducted their trials that they were getting wrong data at different system nodes. Then we realized that we needed a data dump to trace the data.

However, we had only one engineer who was known for his attitude and arrogant personality, and he alone did FPGA coding for the whole company. So I invited the man, Arthur Tucker, to a meeting we spent persuading him to add a patch to his firmware to provide us three trigger points so the system would dump the data when the trigger went off.

After resisting for a while, he added the patch to his firmware. And when the test engineer resumed the test, the trigger went off, the light at the second system node began to flash, and the system printed the data.

Right out of the gate, I was at a disadvantage: first, I had no access to the system software, and second, I had not studied the system data-transfer protocol. Then I realized "the job of a leader is to guide and direct his team, for there lies the productive power of teamwork."

So we proceeded to review the data dump. It was relatively easy for us to discover the point at which the problem started. But the cause would gnaw and chew at us for days. By Friday, our discovery had made its way around to the ears of the executive staff. So on Monday, after the staff meeting, the vice president, Mr. Sweeney, and the director, Mr. Kamath, came to my office.

"That was a kick-ass job, Chuks," Mr. Sweeney said. "I want your team to take ownership of the problem resolution. Let me know if you need any help."

Now we had a new mission, so we went back to the data dump— my team and me. We reviewed the dataflow several times, but could not find the cause. Then we shifted to the data transmission protocol. We had meetings, sometimes three times in one day. After three weeks, we came up empty just as the management was getting anxious because customers were expecting delivery of the system they had ordered.

Meanwhile, the vice president kept asking my boss, Mike, the status of our assignment.

"They are working very hard at it, sir," he answered each time.

One day we took copies of the data dump home. I studied it all night without finding any problem. But when I got to work the next morning, a member of the team, Ron, was waiting for me beside the receptionist's desk. So immediately I walked in, he said, "Chuks, could you come to the cafeteria for a cup of coffee?"

"I don't drink coffee, Ron," I said.

"OK, a cup of orange juice."

"I would like apple juice. Who is buying?"

"You are," he said.

When I joined Ron, Matt had not arrived yet, so we left a message at the front desk for him to join us in the cafeteria when he arrived. A short time later, he joined us and ordered a cup of coffee and toast.

"I found the offending beast," Ron said.

"What did you find?" Matt asked.

A MATTER OF FAITH

"Look at the dump," Ron said. "Node C did not raise the flag for node D after extracting its data, so all the data from that node downstream got ignored. That's a violation of the protocol."

"I saw that node C stripped the flag, but I wasn't sure that it was supposed to raise the flag after extracting its data," Matt said.

"You guys did better than me. I couldn't find any problem," I said.

"That's because they don't use flags where you come from," Ron teased.

"Good job. I will schedule a meeting with the software manager at nine o'clock in the conference room B," I said.

We met again at nine o'clock with the software manager and pointed the problem out to him, so he sent Ben to join us. And then we went over the bug with him.

After lunch, we met again. By that time, Ben had made changes to the software, so we went to the test lab and upgraded the system software. Then the test team ran their test, and the system worked correctly. So I invited my boss, Mike, to the test lab, to witness the test. Later that afternoon, we demonstrated the trial for Mr. Kamath.

The following morning, Mr. Kamath convened an emergency staff meeting and invited my team to discuss the status of our assignment. I let Ron explain the nature of the problem, Matt the steps we took to resolve the issue and Ben the changes he made to the system software.

"Chuks, can you ask the integration team to set up the system?" the VP said. "We will meet you in the lab to witness the test together."

Ron, Matt, Ben, and I went to the test lab while the system was already running, so we told the testing team to idle it until the staff got to the lab. The senior test engineer turned the system off, and then we waited for the staff to arrive. One hour later, they came and stood around the system. Then, Steve, the senior test engineer, turned the system on and began the test. The staff watched all the nodes as the green light went on at each node and the system printed out the arriving data. Then Steve showed Mr. Sweeney the data transmitted to each node and the data printed out at each node, and all the data matched.

"Steve, run the test for a few days, and let me have the result by Friday," the VP said and shook everybody's hand and left the lab.

The following day, first thing in the morning, Mike came to my office, stretched his legs out on top of my desk, and reclined.

"You are the new star in this company," he said. "That's an incredible job you did."

"Wrong! There is no star on the job, just a team of workers, and their managers," I said.

In August 1997, ADC had another major problem. BellSouth had bought the HFC system. It worked for a few days and crashed. Mr. Sweeney dispatched field service engineers to Atlanta to resolve the issue, but after a week, they could not get it to work. Then he sent a team of system engineers to Atlanta; they spent a week there, and they too did not make any headway.

Then at the staff meeting, Mike suggested to the vice president to send me to Atlanta to evaluate the problem.

"It sounds like a brilliant idea," the VP said. "But I am concerned that we've had field service and system engineers down there, and they didn't even know what was going on. But when we brought the system back to our facility, it worked, and then when we sent it back, it crashed again. What do you think Mr. Chuks can do down there?"

"I am not sure, but I believe he will bring back valuable information," Mike said.

"OK, send him, but I don't want him to spend more than a day," the VP said. "Tell Liz to make his trip arrangements for Wednesday."

On Wednesday, I arrived at the BellSouth facility in Atlanta at nine o'clock just as the employees were coming to work. When the technical support manager arrived, we met in the cafeteria.

"Hi, my name is Jonathan," he said.

"Chuks Ndukwe," I replied.

"Let me get my breakfast before we go to the equipment room," he said. "Do you want anything?"

"No, thank you. I ate already."

"No problem," he replied.

He ordered French toast and two scrambled eggs, and then we sat down to wait for his order.

"Are you sure you don't want anything?" he inquired again.

"I am sure. Thank you anyways," I said.

A MATTER OF FAITH

I picked up the paper on the table and began to read the news until he finished his breakfast.

"Let's go and tackle the beast," he said.

"That's not the first thing I want to do," I said.

"What are you here for then?" he asked. "I'm tired of people coming here every day without a clue as to what to do. We are losing revenue from this crap."

"I understand," I said. "you and I could get the system going today, but we have to diagnose the problem first. Who was working on the system when it stopped working?"

"I was," he said.

"Great, tell me what you were doing," I said.

"I was updating customer features when suddenly the system became unresponsive," he said. "I powered the system down and powered it back up, and it hasn't worked since then."

"Whose modem are you using to manage the system?"

"We are using the USRobotics' Courier modem," he said.

"OK, let's go to the equipment room and take a look at the switchgear," I said.

When we got to his switch room, I took a seat beside him while he worked the workstation.

"Turn everything off," I said.

He turned the system and the modem off, and then we waited for one minute.

"Turn the system on," I requested.

He turned the system on again, and then we waited for a few seconds.

"OK, turn the modem on and enter the wake-up command."

"What is that?" he asked.

"AT command."

"Ouch! I forgot."

"That's OK. What did you get?"

"OK."

"Enter ATA. What did you get?"

"I hear a tone."

"That's the answer tone. OK, type AT&T. What do you get?"
"Self-test in progress."
"Type AT&R. What did you get?"
"Resetting."
"We are almost there. Type AT&RST. What do you get?"
"Restoring the previous settings," he said.

It was almost time for lunch, so we went to the cafeteria and grabbed something to eat, and went right back to work.

"OK, you can run your system now," I said.

He entered a load command to download the system software for self-test which the system passed.

Finally, I gave him the telephone number to call Mr. Sweeney's office at ADC.

"I know this number by heart," he said, "I've been dialing it for three weeks."

He dialed the number, and Mr. Sweeney's secretary answered.

"Hello, can I speak to Mr. Sweeney?" he asked.

"Hold on for a minute," she said.

"Hello, this is Sweeney," the VP said.

"Mr. Sweeney, this is the annoying Jonathan at BellSouth," he said. "I have good news; the system is working again, and I have the guy you sent this morning here with me. Do you want to speak to him?" Jonathan asked and gave me the phone.

"Mr. Chuks, what's going on?" The VP inquired.

"Sir, Jonathan, and I have gotten the system working again," I said.

"Do you care to tell me what was wrong, or wait until you come back?" he asked.

"Till I come back, sir," I said.

"OK," he said. "Have a safe flight back."

Immediately when I boarded the plane and sat down, I began to write my trip report, which I finished around midnight after my return home. The first thing the following morning, I gave the report to Mr. Sweeney's secretary, Miss Liz Ryan. Then after lunch, Mr. Sweeney called an emergency staff meeting and invited me while I was in my office doing calculations to determine the line impedance for a Swedish line card.

A MATTER OF FAITH

"Mr. Chuks, can you come to my conference room?" He asked.

"In a minute, sir," I said.

"Do you mean right away?"

"Yes sir, I am on my way," I said, recognizing he did not like my answer.

When I got to his conference room, the staff had some drinks, muffins, and cookies.

"Come in and sit down, and help yourself," he said.

So I sat down and had a corn muffin and apple juice.

"I called this meeting to discuss your trip report," he said. "First of, this is the first time I've received a trip report from an engineer in this company. Second, your report is straightforward, but I want you to summarize the whole event for us."

"Sir, the summary is that nothing was wrong with the switchgear," I said. "The problem was an incorrect configuration of the modem they use to manage it.

"That summary is critical," he said. "Liz, I want you to get it in writing from Mr. Chuks because I intend to transmit it to the president of BellSouth."

As I stood up to leave, he continued.

"Sit down, Mr. Chuks; we are not quite done yet. If there is no objection, I would like Mr. Chuks to join the staff meeting on Mondays."

"I fully second the vice president's motion," Mr. Kamath said.

Therefore, I began to attend the staff meetings on Mondays. The annual Christmas party was looming large. The party was held in the company's conference room, with several restaurants catering to the party. Management dished out some awards to top-performing employees for the year as the highlight of the evening.

Meanwhile, I was not sure of attending the party, because my girlfriend, Doreen, and I had two minor children at home, and we did not have anybody to watch them. But as the night of the party drew closer, I came under pressure by Uma and Mike to attend, so I bought a fitting black suit for the occasion.

Chuks I, Ndukwe

On Friday, a day before the party, Doreen's coworker, Eva, volunteered to babysit for us, so we scrambled, and found a beautiful dress for Doreen to wear.

On Saturday, in the evening of the party, when Doreen and I arrived at the company's building that was located at 125 White Water Drive in Minnetonka, two miles from our house the parking lot was full of cars and people were still arriving for the event—all dressed up like superstars. We entered the conference room and found Uma, Mike, and their wives already seated and waiting for us.

Then the vice president arrived. As he entered the hall, music began to play. Servers strolled around and served all kinds of drinks; Doreen had gin and orange juice, and I had Pepsi. After cocktails, the servers served different types of food; I had flounder and rice, and Doreen had lobster, a baked potato, and vegetables. It took hours for the employees to finish their meals.

After dinner, the DJ played soft music, mostly Western. The bartenders came around again and refilled our glasses. When the caterers finished clearing the tables, the vice president took to the podium and began:

"I want to welcome every member of the ADC family to this annual award party," he said. "We gather every year to celebrate our hard work for the year and give out a few awards. The highest award we give out every year goes to one employee who made the most impact on the operation of this company—somebody who earned not only the respect of his or her peers but that of the staff and our customers as well. For years, this award has gone to an engineer of Far-Eastern descent, but this year we have an employee who comes from the continent of Africa. He was instrumental in solving most, if not all, of the problems this company was having before his arrival. The amazing thing is the ease with which he did it. The day this employee came for an interview, the office was closed. There were six inches of snow on the ground on top of layers of ice, and the temperature was twenty-five degrees below zero. When I looked out of my window, I saw a car sliding all over the parking lot. He steadied his car and walked to the main door, and found the door locked. So I went to the front door and let him inside—covered with snow. He dusted the snow off and walked into the building. The effort he made to get to ADC that day made me like him even before his interview started. Uma and I met with this man and concluded that he was an extraordinary engineer. I can tell we were right for not letting him go. Where is Uma? Come up here and tell us about this man who is the recipient of ADC's top award for this year." He concluded and took his seat.

"Good evening. I am Uma Kamath, the director of the line card department," he said. "You have heard a lot about one of the engineers who work for me. He is a man who loves challenges. We are all aware of the problems we had for months regarding the malfunctioning of our system. This man took on the challenge and resolved the problem with a team of three other engineers. We had another problem with the operation of our system in Atlanta. We worked on it for three weeks without success before the vice president sent this man. Do you know that he fixed the problem in less than four hours? I am proud to announce that this year's Key Contributor Award goes to my department and to a deserving engineer of African descent, Chuks I. Ndukwe."

As it's often the case in instances such as the moment, I had mixed emotions, among which was humility and undeserving of the praise the director and the vice president piled on me. Still, I got up, went to the podium, and received the award. I was surprised to get the award, and so I simply thank the VP, Uma, Mike, and the employees for the honor.

I had the habit of sharing every bit of good news with my children. So the first thing I did the following morning after breakfast was to lie on the couch and call Brockton, Massachusetts, to speak to them—but their number had been disconnected. I called all my friends; they too did not know where my ex had taken them. I was gripped by a pounding headache and fear.

As a result, I went outside to walk around and calm down. Although I did not go far from the house, when I wanted to go home, I forgot how to get back. Finally, I made it home without knowing how it happened and then I called Brockton again. The number was still disconnected. So I called my relatives in New Jersey, and they too could not tell me where my children were.

Now, my head simmered like a pot of boiling water on the stove, on the Sunday morning breakfast, for brewing hot tea. So I went inside the bedroom, and leaned on the headboard as my headache had gotten to a boiling point and about to explode—I could not lay down.

Grasping for anything to take my mind off my children, I turned the TV on and found that the replay of O. J. Simpson's trial was on. While I was watching it, I decided not to go anywhere to look for my children to avoid unexpected fallout. Then I sad, "I will leave it in God's hand as a matter of faith, he will lead me to my children."

I went back to the living room and tried to play some records, but even the ones I loved did not sound good at all. Obviously, I was in a different world at that moment—a world where nothing and nobody meant anything anymore; I did not give a rat's ass. I remember trying to eat foo-foo that evening but the egusi soup, which tasted delicious the last time I ate it did not have any taste. Eventually, I ate Campbell's chicken soup because nothing else could get down my throat—even though I hated chicken soup. Then I lay down.

The following morning, my headache had gotten worse, and my eyes had swelled up. Still unable to shake off the thoughts about my children, I called the police department in Brockton and inquired whether there had been an accident report involving a black lady and her three daughters.

"Sir, we haven't had such a report in more than a year," the officer said.

The best antidote for my headache was that piece of information—that there had not been a report of an accident involving a black woman and her three daughters.

Still, I could not go to sleep. Instead, I just lay down and tortured my mind with conflicting thoughts and wishes that would never materialize

One day, when I was preparing a report on the project I had just completed, I got a call from a gentleman, Jim Reeves, the president of Common Agenda. He wanted to set up an interview for me with Lucent Technologies in New Providence, New Jersey I had never heard of before.

"What's their main product?" I asked.

A MATTER OF FAITH

"They are one of the leading manufacturers of an Internet gateway, VOIP," he said.

For one thing, I had been longing to join such a company for a long time, so I agreed to attend the interview. Therefore, Jim set up the meeting for me. A few days later, I got a call from the office of the director of the PathStar division at Lucent Technologies, Mr. A. Sarath.

"Hi, my name is Helen. I am calling from Lucent Technologies to confirm your appointment for an interview," the caller said.

"Yes, I will be there," I said.

"OK, I am sending you a round-trip ticket," she said. "You can pick it up at the check-in desk of United Airlines."

On the day of the interview, I flew to New Jersey and got the job.

Chapter 9
Sad Ending

Beginnings are usually scary, and endings are usually sad, but it's everything in between that makes it all worth living.

Bob Marley

The first time I set foot inside Lucent Technologies' world headquarters, which used to be AT&T, was when I came for the interview. At the center of the lobby were executive couches in sections to allow for intimate conversations flanked by a beautiful lounge to the left and to the right was a gallery of telecommunication inventions dating as far back as the invention of the telephone. The receptionist was just by the stairs overlooking the lobby. The security office was way back to the left, watching everybody and everything that passed through the entrance and exit doors, while the second-floor balcony circled the lobby.

I could see people walking in and out of their offices and others looking down to watch out for the arrival of their guests. The outside was a beautiful landscape with several sections of parking lots, each larger than the mall and full of vehicles of all makes and models.

Honestly, it was intimidating. The mere thought of working there and the fear of not being hired clashed like a train wreck. Luckily, the interviewing manager walked up to me.

"Hi, are you Chuks Ndukwe?" he asked.

"Yes, I am," I replied.

"My name is John," he said. "Please follow me."

We walked up to the stairs and along a winding hallway to the PathStar department. Then John showed me around the lab where a microscope stood at the corner and other equipment I had never heard of before set up in sections. Next, we walked back along the same

A MATTER OF FAITH

hallway to the cafeteria for tea and coffee and walked back—good morning exercise.

Then the interview began followed by handoff from one executive to another until every one of them had a chance at questioning me, and then the engineering crew interviewed me for two hours. During the interview, I kept getting the usual questions "how much are you asking for in terms of salary?" As always, I declined to discuss my salary; instead, I told John to make me an offer when I got home.

After the interview, I had a warm feeling based on the friendly vibes I got from the engineers who escorted me to the parking lot.

Few days after my interview, I got a call from Mr. Sarath. We chatted for a while between *hold-on* and *I'm-backs* and reached an acceptable offer. So I gave my two weeks' notice to ADC and joined Lucent in the summer of 1998.

Before I left Minnesota, Lucent arranged for a moving company to move my belongings to New Jersey and for me to stay at the Best Western Hotel across the street from the office at 1600 Mountain Avenue, Murray Hill, until I found an apartment or a house to buy.

I reported for work on Monday and went straight to a weekly meeting presided over by the chief technical officer, Mr. Phil Winters. He was familiar with every project the department was working on, and he was also the director of Bell Labs' software research department.

Two weeks later, my manager, John gave me an assignment; to design a timing-distribution board for the PathStar system which I began by developing the design specifications—the only way I knew and had started projects by.

Phil presided over the weekly meeting when there was an important matter to discuss or a pressing issue to resolve. He was the most respected and most feared executive. Three weeks after I had my project, he presided over a meeting spent discussing my document *Timing Distribution Design Specifications*. At the beginning of the meeting, he demanded updates on every project and then he turned to me and inquired, "Yes, Mr. Ndukwe, how is the system timing board going?"

"I've completed the first phase," I said.

"OK, tell us about the first phase," he demanded.

Since I had done my research and found all the parts I intended to use in the design, their prices, availability, and their specifications, I described the plan—laid everything on the table, and went over the design schedule. And then I concluded by saying that "I will start the implementation phase if the management approves the technology."

"See me after the meeting," he said.

So after the meeting, I went to see Phil in his office.

"Come in, Chuks. You did a fantastic job with that specification. The job is half-done. Hand it over to John Parks," he said. "I have a group of engineers in the demo room who do not know what they are doing down there. I want you to take over the project after lunch and get that system working."

So then, I went to the demonstration room after lunch and saw four engineers sitting in front of the PathStar system, trying to originate a call from one socket and answer the call on another. When I went home that evening, I weighed a few options on how to join the engineers, who had been working on the system for some time, without seeming to be a condescending smartass.

"How bad could it get? After all, I am doing what Phil wants me to do," I thought.

When I arrived at the office the following morning, I went to the cafeteria and found Prasad, Nikhil, Yan, and Andrew having breakfast. So I joined them with my oatmeal and toast.

"Do you think we can get the system working today?" I inquired about indicating my intention of joining the group.

They flat out ignored me and continued with their conversation. Trifling arrogant sons of bi*ches. It became evident that it would be an unfriendly situation, so I had to get to the system before them.

Coming back, they found me entering a command on the keyboard with a telephone handset on my ear, but I was not getting any sound as specified in the test procedure. So I took the document with me and made a copy for myself. When I came back to the demo room, Prasad snatched the paper from me and asked me to stand aside and watch them. Then I went to report the matter to Phil.

A MATTER OF FAITH

"The group you asked me to work with doesn't want me there," I said.

"I did not ask you to work with them," he said, "I expect you to elbow your way in and take over the damn project."

Next, I took the test procedure, the socket map, and the time-slot memory address to my office and studied them. Then I went back to Phil's office and told him "I would like to make changes to the test procedure."

"Why?" He asked.

"The test should start with verification of the data path," I said, "but this test procedure does not specify that."

"See Ken Thompson," he said.

When he said that, my eyes popped wide open, I could not believe he was sending me to an icon, the author of the C programming language textbook I had used in college. I did not know how to approach him; I must confess I was very intimidated. But after moving reluctantly and dragging my feet, I went to see Ken and told him what I was suggesting in terms of modifying the test procedure.

"That's a brilliant idea," he said. "How much do you know about software coding?"

"I am a software and hardware engineer. Actually, we used your book on C programming language in class," I said.

"I can give you the DSP coefficients for the signals, and you can do it yourself," he said.

"I am not on the Babine server," I said, "I am doing hardware at the moment."

"OK, come back after lunch," he said.

During lunch, I informed the engineers of my intention to modify the test procedure and inflicted looks of contempt upon their faces.

"I'm changing the test procedure," I said. "The current procedure is flaky."

"Aren't you the hardware engineer who was hired just last week?" Prasad inquired.

"Yes, I am. My name is Chuks I. Ndukwe," I said.

"How do you know what we are doing?" he asked.

"Maybe we should ask Phil that question," I said.

When I finished my lunch, I went to Ken's office as he had just finished burning the new EPROM. So I went to the demo room with it and took the whole chassis apart.

I realized that the best way to fight disrespect, insult, or arrogance on the job is to thrive where insulting characters have failed. With that in mind, I waited for the group to come back to the demo room and watch me replace the EPROM and put the chassis together.

When they came back, I began to put the chassis together as they lost themselves in disbelief and watched, not saying anything but just watched.

There are times when, because I am black, I let insults slide. But that time, I wanted to make a statement, not with words but with actions. So I pushed the router back into its slot. I powered the system on and went from the first socket to the last, issuing commands and listening for the prescribed signals.

When I finished, I found three sockets that were not producing any signals, then I said, "We are almost there."

Then I went back to Ken and told him what I had found.

"That's fantastic. Come back in thirty minutes for a new EPROM," he said.

Instead of thirty minutes, I waited for one hour before going back to Ken's office, returned to the demo room with a revised EPROM, and continued the test. This time all the sockets gave out signals, as they were required.

"The system is working now," I told the group and reported to Phil.

"I want you to show me how it is working," he said.

Like a soldier who has just accomplished his mission, I marched to the demo room as Phil followed and demonstrated the testing.

"That's brilliant. I knew you could do it," Phil said.

Except when I am on a trip, I never went for more than three days without eating African food [foo-foo]. And at that moment, I had gone way past that limit, so I called my nephew, Chima E. Chima.

"Hey, Chima, I can't stand this hotel food anymore. How far do you live from New Providence?" I asked.

"It's about thirty minutes drive," he said.

A MATTER OF FAITH

"Give me directions to your house," I said. "I will stay with you until I find an apartment."

My actions may seem odd to the reader or as if I were imposing. But for me, though, having grown up in Nigeria, where family means a great deal, the elder member of the family reserves the right to impose—just a little; once in a while—just for love's sake.

Chima gave me directions to his address on Lincoln Avenue in Newark, New Jersey. Then I told him that I would call him the next day before leaving the hotel.

"I will be home at eight o'clock," he said.

"OK, I will see you around nine," I replied.

The following day, I called Chima up, as he had just walked through the door.

"Hello, this is Chima," he said.

"Chima, it's me. I am on my way," I said.

I followed his directions and arrived at his apartment around eight forty-five while he was in the kitchen cooking, so I joined him in the kitchen. Chima was a little kid when I left Nigeria, so I still had that image of him standing on the veranda, watching family members come home from the market, not the grown-up who was comfortable around the kitchen.

So we cooked together, bumping into each other, looking for a pepper, salt, and whatever. Then after dinner, we washed dishes together. I could sense Chima almost screaming at me, "Uncle, get out of the kitchen," but he did not, out of respect.

To be candid about it, I was delighted to share the kitchen with him as we did. The reason being, Chima lost his older brother around the same time I lost my sister and judging from the immense sadness I felt, I had a sense of what he felt, and as young as both of us were, I did not know how to console him, so I had stayed away from him until then.

Anyways, after dinner, Chima told me that he was traveling to Nigeria to see some beautiful girl he wanted to marry, and so he left me alone in his apartment and went to Nigeria the following day

One week after Chima had left for Nigeria, I found an apartment in Linden. A few days later, I received a call from the moving company to schedule a date to deliver my belongings. So when Chima returned, he and Ebere helped me to move my things to the apartment.

On Monday, after the weekly meeting presided over by Phil, he told me to get ready to travel to Naperville, Illinois, to help debug a new system that division had designed for us.

"Can you leave tonight?" Al asked.

"I can leave right now if necessary," I answered.

"OK, let me call Connie," he said.

He called Connie, Lucent's travel manager and said to her, "Hi, Connie, Chuks is in my office right now, I will send him over for his travel arrangements. He is leaving at five from Newark to Chicago this evening."

"I want you to pay close attention to how they debug the system so you can work on it with minimal assistance," Phil said.

"Go and see Connie," Al said. "By the way, do you have a credit card?"

"No, sir, not yet," I answered.

"See me when you finish with Connie," he said.

Getting back to Al's office, he gave me a credit card to travel with and cautioned that the daily expense limit was two hundred dollars.

Meanwhile, Connie had made my reservations at Days Inn, at 1350 East Ogden Avenue in Naperville and also a ticket for a rental car with Avis Rent a Car.

When I arrived at O'Hare airport, I picked up a car at Avis's office, drove to Naperville, and checked in at Days Inn. Then on Monday, I reported to Lucent's facility at 2000 Naperville Road, as the manager of the hardware development department, Mr. Hinterlong, was waiting for me. So I followed him to his office where we chatted before he invited two other engineers to join us.

"Mr. Ndukwe, here are my two engineers with whom you will be working, Dave and Vince," he said.

I spent four weeks with Dave and Vince debugging the system that ultimately became mine. On the day I left Naperville, we had some drinks at the hotel before Mr. Hinterlong, Dave, and Vince went home. Then I spent the night writing my trip report and returned to New Jersey on Saturday.

A MATTER OF FAITH

On Monday, during the weekly meeting, Phil gave me a new system-description document and said, "I want you to review this document and come up with a better design."

I began to write my product design specifications immediately, describing the existing design and its limitations, the new design, its extended capabilities, and the new parts I intended to use in its implementation, their availability, and costs. Once I had finished the design-specification document, I distributed it and called a meeting to review it. At the meeting, I went through the document page by page and described the new design concept.

"Why don't you design a board with a hundred and twenty-eight channels instead of a board with two hundred and fifty-six channels?" John Parkes asked.

"That will render the system channels limited," I answered.

"The crystal oscillator you chose is not a good part," Chin Thomas said.

"If you have a better part," I said, "please forward the specification to me, and I will be happy to review it. Can you tell us why the oscillator is a bad part?"

"It has a high jitter level," Chin said.

"That can be taken care of by good design practice," I replied.

I had heard that Phil provided design architecture for every design, so after the meeting, I went to his office and requested the design architecture from him.

"Phil, I am ready to start my design," I said. "Could you provide me with the design architecture?"

"You don't need any help from me. You can do it," Phil said.

Feeling flattered and a little jittery, I told my manager, John, what Phil had said.

"I am not surprised. John is impressed by your engineering ability," he said. "Go ahead and do the architecture, and give it to me first. I will run it by him and get his feedback."

I worked on the product architecture for two weeks and handed it over to John as he had requested.

"I think you nailed it," he said. "I will let Phil take a peek. See me after lunch."

Therefore after lunch, when I went to see John, he said, "I showed it to Phil, and he took it from me without a word. I think he liked it."

Then I made another copy and gave it to him. In the next Monday meeting—as always, Phil demanded updates on all project statuses. When he got to me, he said, "Chuks, I've reviewed your architecture; you can go ahead with it."

Adrenaline surging through the blood in every vein—in my body, I realized I have earned the recognition I deserved in the High Tech industry. Evidently, after the meeting, other engineers came to my office and asked for a copy.

"This is the first time Phil has asked any one of us to continue with a design without providing his own design architecture," Chin told me.

A few weeks later, I completed the schematics, distributed copies, and scheduled a review meeting, presided over by Phil himself.

"How long will it take you to complete the project?" Phil asked.

So I handed him my project schedule and said,

"As you can see, I am ahead of my schedule by two weeks, so I think the design will be completed in two months."

"This is what I want every project to look like," he said. "I think you are on a roll."

At the next Monday meeting, Phil announced that John had quit and a new manager, Dr. Chris Autry, would be taking over. A week later, Chris arrived and took over the management of the department. Chris had just received his doctorate degree in electrical engineering from the University of North Carolina. The news was that he had done co-op at Lucent when he was a graduate student. After the meeting, he made his rounds and talked to every engineer.

On Friday, I continued to work on my board way past the closing time while other engineers had left the lab and gone home. Chris walked in, just as I was about to lock the door.

"How is it going, Chuks?" he inquired.

"It is going pretty well. This is the second board I've gotten to work in two weeks," I said.

Just to prove it, I originated a call from my board to him.

A MATTER OF FAITH

"Hello," he said as he picked up the phone. "Who is calling?" We talked on the phone; then we hung up and went home.

Then on Monday, before the weekly meeting, I went to the lab to continue to debug the third board, but after the meeting, the board began to smoke when I turned it on. As I walked to my office past Chris's office, I heard Norm Lutz telling Chris that he could get my board to work.

"I will give him more time. After all, he is well ahead of his schedule," Chris said.

I pretended that I did not hear what Norm said and kept walking to my office to get the parts list for the board, and then I went back to the lab and continued to probe the circuit board to find the cause of the smoke. After examining a few parts, I found one resistor that had fused up. When I inspected both sides of its placeholder, I did not see any damage done to the board itself.

Therefore, I replaced the resistor and continued to debug the board. Later in the afternoon, Chris walked into the lab and inquired "How is the debugging going Chuks?"

I simply placed a call from the board to the phone next to Chris. Then Chris picked the phone up and said, "Hello."

"Chris, this is Chuks," I said, smiling. "I am calling from the smoked board."

"What was wrong with the board?" he asked.

"It was a freaking resistor of the wrong value."

"How many boards do you have left?"

"Three boards. I should be done by the end of next week."

"Great, good job," he said.

After Chris left the lab, the other engineers gathered around my workbench.

"Did you look at the signal coming out of that crystal oscillator?" Chin asked.

"Let's look at it," I said.

So Chin put a probe on it, and the signal was clean and reliable. Then he said, "It wasn't this good when I used it."

"Did you place an outside call?" Norm asked.

"Yes, I called California," I said.

I finished debugging the boards and released the project to the system-testing department ahead of schedule.

Two weeks later, Chris dashed into my office and said.

"Chuks, we discussed your project in the staff meeting this morning," he said. "The boards passed the final test. We can release it to the factory for production."

I recognized right away that I had made a good impression upon Chris. Meanwhile, new companies were springing up all over the United States. Engineers were leaving their companies to join start-up companies.

But on the negative side, the Internet was crashing and taking a long time to recover. Cisco Systems was beating the daylights out of Lucent Technologies because the PathStar system router was unreliable and customers were complaining about it.

The executive staff, Bill, Allen, Phil, Norm, John, and some engineers from Bell Labs had been at it for a while without progress. For some unknown reasons, the software research scholars at Bell Labs claimed that the problem was hardware, so Norm was doing all kinds of things to disprove their claim without success.

One day Chris invited me to his office for a short meeting we spent discussing his trip to North Carolina.

"I've appointed you my delegate," he said. "So you will attend the staff meeting and represent the department on Monday."

"Could I decline?" I joked.

"You can try if you like," he replied. "But as my favorite engineer, I'd advise you not to."

For that reason, we went over the statuses of all the projects in the department and then he gave me instruction on which projects to discuss. Then on Monday morning, I went to the vice president's conference room—scared out of my skull.

When the meeting began, all the managers and directors sat around the shiny oval table as the vice president started the meeting with a brief overview of the current state of the division. Then he went around the table and asked each manager about the statuses of the projects they were working on.

A MATTER OF FAITH

As if he were taking a headcount, he looked around and paused.

"Chris Autry is out of the office for family matters," he said. "But we have his delegate here with us. Mr. Ndukwe, can you tell us what's going on in your department?"

"I will do my best, sir," I joked. "The good news is that my beloved director is here, so if I screw up, he will set me straight. OK, the multimode fiber optics interface was completed and released to manufacturing last Friday. That project was a couple of weeks ahead of schedule. COMDAC continues to work without issues. The T1 board was released to the test and integration group, and Chris is waiting for their feedback. Two engineers, Ben Lange and Moy Dat, are on vacation. Finally, the effort to fix the router is continuing."

"What can you tell us about the ATM interface board?" he inquired.

"I was not advised to discuss that project, sir."

"You might not have been advised to discuss it," he said. "My question is this: Can you tell us what you know?"

"I have no information on that project, sir."

"Can you go and find out what the status is?"

"That would be against my manager's directives, sir."

"OK, I guess we can wait till your manager returns," he said.

"Thank you, sir," I replied.

After the meeting, Mr. Sarath stopped by my office and said, "You did pretty well, Chris would be glad to hear about your encounter with the VP."

Chris was generally pleased to hear about the meeting when he returned. So from that day forward, we met on Fridays after work and discussed project issues and courses of action.

When I arrived at work one Monday morning in June 1999, rumor had it that customers were threatening to return their systems to Lucent because of the poor performance of Lucent's router. There was talk also about HA (high-availability) feature. After the staff meeting, Chris called John Parks to his office to answer questions Phil had asked about the work he did on the new HA system feature.

For one thing, all Internet-gateway-equipment manufacturers bought the embed-computers they used to manage the HA feature from Intel, so the intermittent crashing of the Internet affected every company that implemented the feature.

The HA feature involved two computers, a designated primary, and a secondary, interchanging the system control when one went down to avoid Internet downtime.

Another variation involved two power supplies, a designated primary, and a secondary under the control of one computer. In this case, the embedded Intel computer switches power-supply to the secondary when the primary power supply fails. In either case, the problem could be resolved only in Intel's processor.

The managers and top engineers had had at it day and night for a long time without success. Bell Labs scientists assisted, but they too did not make any breakthroughs.

✳ ✳ ✳

One day, Chris came to my office and said, "Come on, Chuks. Let's go and see the director."

"What did I do?" I asked.

"You will find out in a minute," he said.

When we got to Al's office, he was going over the new weekly schedule.

"Come in and have a seat," Al said. "Yes, what can I do for you?"

"To discuss what I proposed last week," Chris said. "This guy is an experienced manager, a high performing engineer. Moreover, he understands the network from the central office to the customer access point."

"Give me a few days," Al said.

Then two weeks later, an e-mail went out announcing Dr. Chris Autry's resignation and my promotion to manage the department. Adding salt to injury, Phil had left Lucent to start a new company in California. Also, a few days later, four engineers resigned and joined Chris at his new start-up company—Tellium Inc.

A MATTER OF FAITH

Therefore, upon taking over the department, I had lost four experienced engineers and inherited two persistent problems, one of which had existed for two years.

I recognized the urgency of the issues and hired two experienced engineers, Lee Glinski and John Lu, despite their little or no telecommunication experience. However, to mentor them and speed up their understanding of the technology, I assigned two engineers to every project: a primary and a secondary.

Therefore I assigned myself to the existing router problem as the primary project engineer and John Lu as the secondary; Lee Glinski to a new router that would double the speed of the current router as the primary and myself as the secondary, and John Parkes as the primary on the HA feature and myself as the secondary.

So I had my hand in every pot as we began to delve into the heart of the current issues. I borrowed one PathStar system; set it up in the engineering lab and instructed John to hook up oscilloscopes on the critical parts of the power-control circuitry and set up triggers. Then it ran for five days and crashed.

After a thorough review of the events before and after the triggers went off, we found that the two Intel computers in the system that made up the HA feature were in contention with each other, causing the systems to crash. Then we printed out the images of the signals before and after the crash.

Now with the evidence in hand, I invited the Intel engineering manager, Lucent Technologies' managers, and John Parkes to a meeting to discuss the result of our experiment.

When the meeting started, only John Parkes, the Intel manager, Mr. William, and I attended. , we continued the discussion with William telling us the details of the implementation of the HA feature in their computer. He described the functionality and the control mechanism and provided us with the Boolean equation they had employed in its execution. Immediately when he handed the logic table to me, I noticed the problem and drew his attention to a specific point on the table where the entries showed the two power supplies came on at the same time and said "Intel designed contention in the product."

"Can you explain what you mean by your assertion?"

To clarify the situation from the perspective of a non-software engineer, I used an analogy with a dinner party in which either the father or the daughter—not both would get a ticket with the attendee's name-tag on arrival. As a rule, the father was the primary invitee and his daughter the secondary. Moreover, the secondary invitee was allowed in only if the primary did not show up.

In one case, the father arrived alone and had his name written on the name-tag. In another example, the daughter came alone and had her name written on the name-tag.

But in a particular case, the father and his daughter arrived together in the same way as the two power supplies came on together, so I asked, "Who should get preference?" The answer was in the rule.

Setting software aside, we turned to ways of dealing with a similar situation from the perspective of a hardware engineer.

"If that is the cause, we can prove it right away," John Parkes said.

"How do you plan to do that?" I asked.

"We can delay the voltage rise time of one power supply and see how the computers would assign control," he said.

"How long will it take for you to modify the power supply?" I asked.

"It won't take long; believe me," he said.

So we followed John to the lab, and there he turned both systems on simultaneously, and the two systems locked up. Then he made the changes he had recommended and turned both systems on simultaneously again, and this time, the system did not crash. He tried several times, and the systems remained stable.

It was lunchtime by then, so we went to the cafeteria, as all those managers I had invited to the meeting were eating their lunches and chatting. When we went back to the meeting, we agreed that Intel would fix the Boolean equation as a long-term solution while we continued with our temporary fix. To prove the fix, John gave the modified system to the test department to initiate a disruptive test-run to crash the system.

"Why do you want to do that?" the test manager asked.

"I will tell you after the crash," I said.

A MATTER OF FAITH

"Before you start the test, have John Parkes hook up oscilloscopes on the system," I said. "We want to capture the events before and after the crash."

The system ran for two weeks without crashing. Then John added his fix to two other systems that were frequently crashing. After the repair, they stopped crashing too. So at the next staff meeting, the test department manager reported that his systems had not crashed since Chuks and his engineer made some changes to the frames.

"Mr. Chuks, what's going on, and why did it take you so long?" the VP asked.

"Sir, we met with the Intel manager last week to discuss the issue," I said, "during the meeting, I discovered faulty implementation of the HA feature. Intel will implement the long term fix while John Parkes continues with the temporary fixes which are working."

"How long has the system been on a rigorous test?" the VP asked.

"One week," Mr. Duval said.

"Test it for two more weeks," the VP said. "If it continues to hold, do the fixes on all the systems. Chuks, I might want to borrow your engineers to go to the field and make the changes."

"That won't be a problem, sir," I said.

After two weeks of additional rigorous testing, the systems, including some that customers had returned, did not crash, so I sought final instructions from my boss on the matter.

"Sir, the test report shows the fixes holding up," I said. "What's the next step?"

"I would like you to escalate the issue to the executive level," he said, "so that the VP can take it up with Intel and expedite the final implementation."

Therefore, I executed the escalation request after which Lucent Technologies' customers began to take back the equipment they had returned.

However, I still had a router problem. So at the staff meeting, I announced the beginning of the new one-twenty MHz router project in parallel with the redesign of the ailing sixty-six MHz router.

"Lee Glinski will be the primary engineer on the new one-twenty megahertz router, and I will be the secondary engineer," I said. "On the sixty-six megahertz router, John Lu will be the primary engineer, and I will be the secondary. The two routers will share the same platform."

A few weeks later, I called for a design review of the routers after which Mr. Peck sent out me an e-mail and copied the VP and my boss stating:

"This is to inform you that the design you presented this morning for review will not work. I will send you proposals that will help you in your design."

I realized that it would come up at the next staff meeting. So I prepared my response. Just as I had predicted, at the next staff meeting, the VP wanted to know what the e-mail was about.

"Mr. Chuks, have you met with Mr. Peck to discuss the issue he raised?" he asked.

"No sir, we've not met, but I sent him a reply, and I've called him several times for his input or an explanation of what he thought the problem with the design was, but I haven't received his response," I said. "But I have an idea. I will give Mr. Peck a copy of the project database and three PCBs when I receive the six Norm ordered. He can implement his ideas while John and I continue with the project, so we don't lose any time arguing about the design, because I don't have any problem with the design as is."

"That sounds like a good idea, Mr. Chuks," the VP said.

However, Mr. Peck was not present in that meeting, so after the meeting, I called him up, went to his office, and installed the project database on his system. When I received the PCBs, I gave Mr. Peck three for his group to work with.

"What are you going to do if Dick gets the router to work first?" the VP asked at the next meeting.

"I will have John Lu work with Dick's team to get it released," I replied.

While John Lu and Lee Glinski were working on the hardware, I dissected the firmware to figure out its structure. When I finished reviewing the source code, I decided to redesign the whole program and announced my intention in the next meeting.

A MATTER OF FAITH

"Why would you do a thing like that at this late stage of the project when we are talking about testing and integration?" the VP asked.

"I am not touching the original code," I said. "I will be designing new firmware while the current effort is going on. Actually, my design is for the high-speed router."

"Now you are talking," he said.

I changed the design to a hierarchical modular structure, and I decided to seek advice from the software director, Mr. Scordo and said to him:

"Sir, I want to consult with you before I continue to restructure and design new firmware for the new router, the current code is a flat design. It is unwieldy, with no comments. You really have to spend a lot of time to figure out what any part of the code is about. I want to make it hierarchical, modular, and with comments so engineers can understand what they are reading."

"I had no idea that you're a software engineer and such a good one at that," he said. "I rarely hear engineers talking about modular and hierarchical designs. Go ahead."

While I was reviewing signal names and variables, I stumbled over one specific signal a buffer—routed outside the block and back inside, in complete violation of VHDL rules. So I redefined it as in/out and proceeded with my work. I finished the global-signal definition, segregated the code into modules, and compiled it with few syntax errors.

On Thursday, December 23, 1999, I took my work home. On Christmas Day, while my girlfriend and my nephew were watching Christmas festivities on the TV, I worked on my computer trying to debug my code. Then on New Year's Eve, just as the ball was about to descend at Times Square in New York City, I heard my girlfriend, Renee, shout, "Chuks, the ball is about to fall."

"I will be right there," I said.

Before they began to scream, "Happy New Year!" the code compiled error-free. So I ran to the living room and watched the countdown. Then we hugged and wished each other a happy New Year.

On Monday, January 3, 2001, at the staff meeting, the VP wanted to know how the router code redesign was going."

"It is going pretty well, sir," I said. "I worked on Christmas Day and the New Year's to get it completed, just in case you hear that I took two days off. I know my boss wouldn't mind, but yes, I did find something peculiar."

"Would you like to share what you found with us?"

"It would be premature. Give me two weeks," I pleaded.

"No objection," he said.

After the meeting, I gave the code to Lee and John to run it in their own routers. They burned the EPROM and popped it in their boards. After probing a few critical signals that had caused problems in the past, everything looked stable.

"John, run the sixty-six megahertz router in the PathStar system overnight," I said "and Lee, run the new router at sixty-six megahertz on the bench fixture overnight,"

Simply stated, both routers worked well. Therefore, I sent John's board to the testing department for a final test while Lee and I continued to work on his board to get it to run at one-twenty MHz, but the closest we got was one hundred MHz.

One week later, I called Mr. Duval for the report on the board I had given him to test.

"Hey, Pat, can I have the test report on that sixty-six megahertz router board I gave you one week ago?" I asked.

"I don't issue reports on unofficial tests, but your board has not failed since we put it on test one week ago," he said.

"Could you do me a favor?" I asked.

"What is that, Chuks?"

"Mention it in the staff meeting?" I requested.

"No problem," he said.

During the next staff meeting, the VP asked for the status of the router.

"Dick, how's the router project?"

"We are working on it, but it is not looking good," Mr. Peck said.

"Pete, any news?" the VP asked.

A MATTER OF FAITH

"Bill, I am getting angry calls from customers regarding the router," Pete said.

"Pat, what's up? I guess you don't have any test going," the VP said.

"Chuks' sixty-six megahertz router has been on test for one week, and it is holding up pretty well," Pat said.

"What do you mean by that?" the VP asked.

"Chuks gave me one of John Lu's boards to test, and it's been running for a week without errors," Pat said. "It never ran more than two days without crashing before."

"That is excellent news," the VP said. "OK, Mr. Chuks, what do you have for us today?"

"I have two major announcements," I said. "First John Lu's boards are working very well in the system environment, so I will be releasing them to the test department after getting instructions from my boss. Second, the new one-twenty megahertz router is running as good as the sixty-six router at a hundred megahertz, so we can release it as a one-hundred-megahertz router if my boss approves."

"Why do you keep referring to your boss? He is right here. You can ask him; don't be afraid," the VP said.

"I would like to seek his advice in the appropriate setting," I said.

"Did you ever dream of becoming a lawyer?" the VP asked.

"No, sir," I replied.

"You would have done well—maybe not as well as you have as an engineer," the VP said. "Al, could you please tell this man to release the routers?" the VP pleaded.

"As soon as I get his release package," my boss replied.

"In what form is the release package?" the VP inquired.

"The test report and three boards housed in an antistatic package," my boss said.

"Mr. Chuks, do you have your test report and three boards that you can put in an antistatic package?" the VP asked.

"I have only two boards. One is running in the test lab, and I would like to retain one circuit board," I said.

~ 111 ~

"Al, can you release two boards since one is already under test?" the VP asked. "Mr. Chuks can get his boards back from Dick's department and complete work on those. I need some bending of the rules here."

"OK, we will release the boards after this meeting," my boss said.

"All right, Mr. Chuks, you can go now. I am done with you," the VP said. "Get the package ready so Al can sign off on that when he comes back."

So after the meeting, Al signed the release document and sent me over to Mr. Duval's to deliver the release package.

"That was a nice battle you fought with the VP," Pat said.

A week later, I released the one hundred MHz router for testing. Then at the next staff meeting, Pat announced that both the sixty-six MHz and one hundred MHz routers had passed the test, so I executed the final factory release.

Before the meeting adjourned, Mr. Scordo stood up and said, "I would like the staff to stand up and give Mr. Chuks and his department an ovation for the amazing job they've done in a few weeks."

After the release of the routers, Lucent Technologies' customers began to take back not only the routers but the systems they had returned.

As though in a dream, a rumor began to spread that Lucent Technologies' stock was taking a hit on Wall Street because the company had recorded its quarterly earnings incorrectly. A few days later, Lucent conducted a companywide teleconference during which the CEO, Mr. Schacht, took to the podium, and the employees cheered. We could see employees in every location on the TV monitor, cheering with a loud ovation.

"We have experienced a huge decline in our stock price on the stock market," he said. "We made some errors in our accounting methods, and we are taking steps to correct them. The current situation requires restructuring for us to continue to offer an amazing collection of products we have in our portfolio. We will emerge from this ordeal more nimble and better positioned to carry on our mission."

"How deep do you see the restructuring effort?" one employee asked.

A MATTER OF FAITH

"We will go deep enough to meet the current challenge," Mr. Schacht said. "Our goal is to put this company back on the trajectory for growth again."

"What will be the nature of the restructuring you outlined in your speech?" another employee asked. "Will it be disposing of the company's assets or resizing or a combination of the two?"

"We will not be shy of doing both if necessary," Mr. Schacht said. "All right, thank you all for attending."

When I returned to my office, I could not do any work. My engineers came to my office one after the other and sat on anything they could sit on.

"What do you think is going to happen?" John Parkes asked.

"I have no idea," I said.

"We were just recognized a few weeks ago for our outstanding performance," Chin said. "Do you think they will consider that?"

"I do not know," I replied. "I've never seen a situation like this before."

When I got home, my head caught fire, sleep became elusive, and thinking clearly seemed a thing of the distant past.

On Friday, Lucent gave the employees—over forty thousand worldwide four weeks to find another job or file for unemployment benefits.

That was an excellent way of saying "you've been laid off." However, I did not receive a lay off benefit package now.

Chapter 10
They Won't Let Go

Sometimes life's going to hit you in the head with a brick. Don't lose faith. I'm convinced that the only thing that kept me going was that I loved what I did.

~ Steve Jobs

Although I did not receive a lay-off notice the day Lucent laid off its employees; still, I had no reason to think that my job was any more secure than those who'd been advised to look for a job or file for unemployment benefits. In fact, my future at Lucent was in limbo, and that gave me no cause for peace of mind.

Then on Monday, a guy in a suit came to my office as I was chatting with my engineers; still angry from the events of the previous week, I said, "Can I help you?"

"My name is Mark," he said. "I'm a research director at Bell Labs, and I want you to know that I am working on getting you transferred to my department with two of your engineers. Keep that in mind before you think of pursuing other opportunities."

"Can I have your business card in case anything comes up?" I asked.

Mark gave me his business card and told me where his office was located. Two days later, Al confirmed that I would be transferring to Bell Labs with Lee Glinski and John Lu. Now comforted, but not relieved, we began to wait for the official announcement.

A MATTER OF FAITH

When I arrived at work the following day, most employees had given themselves up to brooding. Indeed, nobody gave a rat's ass—nor should they! The game was over, and we had lost—all of us.

After waiting for a long time without getting the official notification of our transfer to Bell labs, we began to send out résumés to different companies.

One day, I got a call from a lady.

"Hello, my name is Melisa Barkan. I am calling from CyberPath," she said. "I am calling to set up your interview. How does next Thursday at ten-thirty grabs you?"

"That sounds good," I said.

"I look forward to seeing you then," she said. "Ask for Melisa when you arrive."

On Thursday, I arrived at CyberPath and reported to the security office.

"Hi, my name is Chuks Ndukwe. I have an appointment with Melisa Barkan," I said.

The security officer paged Melisa, and a few minutes later, she met me in the lobby and led me to the office of the president, Dr. Chai Chun Lin.

"Hello, Chuks. Please come in and have a seat," Dr. Lin said.

"Thank you, sir," I said and sat down. Then he called the director of engineering, Mr. Zhang Xu.

"Mr. Ndukwe is here," Dr. Lin said. "How are you, Mr. Ndukwe? I suppose you don't recognize me."

"No, sir, have we met before?" I asked.

"I was occupying Mark Hansen's office before I left Lucent to start this company," he said. "I watched you work in the lab under John Tsimaras and Dr. Chris Autry until I left Bell Labs a few weeks after your promotion."

After the interview, he offered me a position of hardware manager and a handsome salary of twenty-five percent more than I was making at Lucent—plus vast stock options and a signing bonus.

Still, I could not get excited. When I returned to Lucent, Lee and John came to my office and sat down to hear about my interview.

"How did the interview go?" Lee asked.

"It was a weird interview," I replied.

"Why?"

"I was offered the job, but I don't feel excited enough to accept it," I said.

"Take the job. This is not the time to pick and choose," Lee said.

Despite Lee's advice, I failed to whip up even a tiny bit of excitement about the job. When I went home, rather than share the news with my girlfriend, I felt a sense of betrayal. Then I realized that I did what I had never done before—discuss a salary during an interview. And that was definitely a breach of my principle of not negotiating salary during an interview. So when I went to work the next day, I sought to remedy the situation and went to Dr. Hansen's office to find out from him what was holding up my transfer.

"I am waiting for Mr. Proetta's approval," he said.

"I have been offered a position at CyberPath, and I am in the process of making a decision," I said.

"I know Dr. Lin," he said. "He used to occupy my office. I will match whatever offer he makes. I will not let you go. Let's go and see my secretary and find out where the process stands now."

Sensing that I was about to resign, he led the way to Bell Labs' administrative office, and there he spoke to Miss Cathy Blanchard and inquired, "Cathy, about Chuks Ndukwe, what's holding up his transfer to Bell Labs?"

"I am still waiting for Mr. Proetta's signature," she said.

"Get him on the phone now," Dr. Hansen said. "I want to speak to him."

She called Mr. Proetta's office.

"Liz, this is Cathy at Bell Labs. Dr. Hansen wants to speak to Bill about Mr. Chuks's transfer authorization," she said and gave Mark the phone to speak to Mr. Proetta.

"He's been away for a few weeks," Liz said. "I will bring Mr. Chuks's file over after lunch. The request has been signed."

"How about the offer CyberPath made me?" I inquired.

"I will match the offer," he said. "You and your guys can start moving the lab equipment in your lab over to mine. Here is the key."

A MATTER OF FAITH

"Why don't we use my lab?" I said. "It is closer to your office and mine, and it has everything we need to do our job."

Then I left Dr. Hansen's office and invited Lee and John to my office and told them "We are officially members of Bell Labs, and we will retain our lab, and what I like the most is that he will match the offer CyberPath gave me."

The next day, we filled out W-9 forms and received official Bell Labs name-tags.

Six months later, my salary had not changed. Therefore, I went to see Dr. Hansen.

"Sir, I want to know why my salary has not changed as you promised," I said.

"Chuks, I did not promise you anything," he said. "I said that I would try to match the offer. I don't think that management will entertain any request like that at this time."

Outraged, I went back to my office and made a copy of the wireless router architecture I was working on and gave it to him. After reading it, he came to my office, sat down, and said, "I hope you're not thinking of quitting, I think it is unwise to submit a request to change your salary amid the dangerous situation the company finds itself. Let's wait until the economic condition improves."

Caught between crying over spilt milk and acting at the drop of a hat, I decided against either and worked for Bell Labs for three more months before I got laid off. For me, that was the moment when the economic crash became real and complete.

Finally, it hit me "Dr. Hansen's failure to pay me what he promised me was indeed a breach of an implied consent agreement." Then I remembered the old man who had sat next to me—inside the train in Chicago once in 1995 while discussing personal issues with his friend. He had said to his friend, "I forgive insults, but abuses, man! I'm intolerant as hell!" Yes, what Dr. Hansen did to me was a clear case of abuse of power.

Therefore, I became enraged and intolerant, so when I went home, I searched through the *Yellow Pages,* and found a lawyer, Mr. Hankridge Waters in East Orange, and called him up.

"This is Attorney Waters' office. Can I help you?" a lady asked.

"Yes, my name is Chuks Ndukwe. I have a case I would like Mr. Waters to review," I said.

"OK, give me your name and telephone number," she said. "I will make an appointment for you to come in and speak to him."

So I gave her my name and telephone number, and she gave me an appointment.

"We charge a consultation fee of two hundred dollars upfront, so bring a check with you," she said.

When I went to see Mr. Waters, I met the lady I had spoken with the previous day.

"Did you bring the consultation fee?" she asked.

"Yes, here is a check for two hundred dollars," I said.

"Have a seat. Mr. Waters will see you in a minute," she said.

All around the office, he had newspaper clips of cases he had won and the award amount of settlements pasted on the wall with prominent ones framed and hung up in a spaced-out decorative fashion. Somehow, I felt confident I was at the right place, and my case would definitely receive a fair hearing.

Shortly, Mr. Waters came out of his office.

"Yes, you are...?" he asked.

"Chuks I. Ndukwe," I answered.

"That's right. Please come with me," Mr. Waters said.

When we got to his conference room, he poured himself a cup of coffee and sat back.

"What can I do for you?"

"I want to file charges against my boss," I answered.

"What is the charge or charges?" he asked.

"Breach of an implied consent agreement," I said.

"OK, can you give me a full account of the nature of the agreement?" he asked. "I mean the witnesses to this agreement, and the name of the defendant?"

I gave him a written account of my transfer from Lucent Technologies to Bell Labs and my job offer by CyberPath that Dr. Hansen had promised but failed to match until Bell Labs laid me off one year later.

"I am seeking one year's payment of the difference between what I was promised and what I was paid," I said. "Plus damages for the pain and suffering he caused me during that period."

He reclined in his executive chair and read the document I had given him three times.

"You have a compelling case," he said. "I will get you what you deserve. Who was your manager at Lucent? By the way, I have a few more cases against Lucent."

"Everything about the case is in the document I gave you, names of defendants, and their positions as well as mine," I said.

"That's right," he said as he glanced through the pages again. "My retainer fee is five thousand dollars up front and thirty percent of the settlement amount if we win the case. I can tell you in advance; this is a winnable case."

So I gave him a check for five thousand dollars and left his office. I felt good, not because I thought that I would win the case but because this black man did not lie down and let a white man walk all over him.

Finally, Mr. Waters filed the case at the Union County Superior Court in Elizabeth, New Jersey.

After months of discovery, the case went to a hearing. During which the judge disclosed that he had interest in Lucent, but my attorney did not ask the judge to recuse himself.

So in the end, the judge dismissed the charges summarily, stating, "Although the charges are founded, there's no evidence to indicate that the defendant acted with malicious intent. The case is dismissed."

Then I went straight to the clerk's office and filled out a form stating my intention to appeal. One week later, I went to Trenton, New Jersey, and filed the appeal pro se.

Still, I had to find a lawyer to argue the case. Therefore, I began to search for one and found an excellent attorney, Mrs. Austin in New Brunswick, New Jersey.

It turned out that earlier in Mrs. Austin's career; she had suffered the same treatment as I did so she could relate to what I felt. So she took the case after reviewing the lower court's ruling.

Finally, she argued the case and won. The Supreme Court sent the case back to the lower court for a jury trial. In some ways, it was a significant step toward justice, in my opinion.

One day, Mrs. Austin invited me to her office for a meeting we had mainly on the strategy for handling the case and in that meeting, she said, "My fear is that Lucent is in a bad financial condition, so they will do their best to drag this case out till they file for bankruptcy. For that reason, we have to wrap this case up quickly."

So before the case went to a jury trial, Lucent settled the case out of court without accepting any wrongdoing.

Chapter 11
Marriage And Children

This was the trouble with families. Like invidious doctors, they knew just where it hurt.

~ Arundhati Roy

The day I first met my estranged wife, Fortune, I had just turned sixteen and at work at the Nigerian Petroleum Refinery in Eleme, Nigeria. I had graduated from technical college and started work there a few months before. In my part of the world, respect for older people is one of the significant Ibo cultural values, and people claim certain unalienable birthrights based on age. Because I was much younger than the men I supervised, I ran errands for them. And in return, they did whatever I asked of them—unwritten laws of social order and mutual understanding.

One bright sunny day, while we were inspecting electrical meters along the pipeline, my men sent me out to a store across the street from the refinery to buy cookies for them. While in the store, I met the girl who worked there and without cause, we clashed over the novel *Young Love* (authored by a nineteen-year-old girl) she was reading. I had read it before and I knew it was about love and sex; it was about the girl's boyfriend, virginity and the loss of it, sex, and betrayal.

She was a high-school student on the Christmas holidays. As it's typical of boys in the transition to adulthood, I invited her to visit me before going back to school. At that time, talking on the phone was not an option because people did not have phones at home.

Following the tradition, girls were married off at an early age, such as fourteen or fifteen—by family arrangements to the wealthy men who had two to three wives and mostly uneducated.

Despite having multiple wives, they lured innocent high school girls with money and gifts, and then they turned around and accused the girls of milking them out of their money. I am not all that naïve to think that none of the girls did some milking—no! Lots of them might have, but it was not a common practice.

For one thing, at the age of twelve, I had formed opinions on many, especially when my mom was fading away, languishing after the death of my sister. As an example, one of the views I formed was that girls are closer to God than boys—angels of God to be specific. How did such a weird opinion come about? You might ask!

Here's what happened: To console mom. I vowed to become her make-believe daughter and do anything her daughter could do for her. But when my village girls heard what I said, they rallied around mom as their own. And not only brought her back to her healthy and cheerful life but also transformed her into a highly spiritual woman.

It was with the appreciation of what the girls did for my mom that I started dating my first girlfriend. I can say for sure; she was not a "milker." From the way, she criticized her mother for wearing makeup, high heels, her sexy appearances, and for chasing after rich men.

How could you not fall in love with a girl like Fortune—if you have a bit of commonsense? Sometimes I said of her mother, "She is a secretary in a major government agency, the port authority, leave her alone." And then she'd say, "That's a dumb thing to say."

To avoid the cycle of separations most couples suffered during the war, we lived together until the end. To stay active, Fortune traveled to war fronts to sell food items to people who fighting displaced from their homes.

The first time she made her trip, she would neither let me buy her the items nor let me give my mother money to purchase the items. "They had to be a gift from your mother's farm," she said.

I suspect the reader might not find this gesture essential, but for me, it was. It revealed her appreciation of my mom's character, spirituality, and of her approval and support of our relationship.

Despite the rampant bombing, she spent five days on the war front. Then she gave me her profits to deposit in our joint account when she came home.

Although the war ripped families apart, on the flip side, it made our relationship stronger. So much so that she wanted us to marry four days

A MATTER OF FAITH

before I departed Nigeria for the United States. Despite my worries about the unknown—the future and the inevitable challenges that could emerge later and destroy our marriage, I agreed.

Still, I had no reason to say no, so I complied—and we got married. A few minutes before I departed Nigeria, I reminded her about the (pullout) unplanned pregnancy prevention technique that I practiced with her and cautioned her to protect herself. "I did it out of deep affection and appreciation of your feminine values," I said, "but if it happens, rest assured, nothing would ever separate us."

Finally, thirty minutes later, on December 9, 1972, I was on my way to the United States.

✣✣✣

The day Fortune, arrived in the United States to join me, it was on a Saturday in 1977. On my way to wait for her arrival at the airport, there was a fatal accident in the Callahan Tunnel, Boston in the outbound lane, while the inbound traffic moved at normal flow. For that reason, the traffic backed up all the way to the city for two hours.

So I arrived at the airport after her plane had already landed and taken off again. Still, I roamed around the terminals a couple of times, hoping to find her waiting for me.

Finally, I got frustrated and went home. But when I opened the door, Fortune was standing right in front of my apartment door, probably expecting me to come out and open the door.

Just as I rushed to embrace her, she pulled back. Then I unlocked the door and moved her trunk inside the apartment, thinking she was mad at me for not showing up at the airport. So I tried to explain what had happened—why we had missed each other at the airport, but she did not pay attention. Eventually, I discovered that she had had a baby a few months earlier. And that is how my marriage I had hoped to be a happy reunion began.

Six months later, she began to attend Roman Catholic GED preparatory classes. Eventually, she gained admission into Boston Community College, which later became a campus of the University of

Massachusetts. Then she got a nurse's aide job, worked the night shift, and went to school during the day. Meanwhile, we decided to start family formation, so I pulled the break on the pullout practice, and a few months later, she got pregnant.

On June 1, 1978, during summer break, her water broke, so our first daughter, Ere, arrived prematurely, but not too early as to cause any alarm.

In many ways, the birth of our daughter Ere gave our marriage a jump-start as it gave us something of mutual importance to enjoy. When I took Fortune to the hospital, women in labor were screaming so loud that I almost cried. However, Fortune had the baby without any problem, yet the doctor kept the baby in the hospital for four days.

My first experience of fatherhood came when I picked the baby up for the first time. She startled a bit and held my thumb so tight with her tiny little hand, as if to say, "Daddy, don't let go." So I kissed her forehead and said, "You are safe now, my dear."

When Fortune went back to school full time early in September, we began a childcare routine that went something like this: She gave the baby a bath in the evening, went to bed, woke up at ten at night, and then to work from eleven to seven in the morning. Then I kept the baby at night, gave her a bath in the morning, took her to the babysitter, picked her up after classes, and took her home. Then her mother took over until she went to sleep at six in the evening.

As you can see, it worked out well for us. A classmate of mine, Anna Cobert, a single mother, introduced me to her babysitter. She waited for me at the babysitter's house every morning, and after classes, we walked together to the project and picked up the babies.

Have you ever heard of that thing about a baby keeping the mother awake all night? Well, I experienced it too.

✳✳✳

One day in June 1979, I found a letter in my study drawer, and to avoid throwing away important document, I read it and found it was all about sending clothes and shoes home for a baby boy. "It can't be Fortune's letter," I thought. So I put it back.

A MATTER OF FAITH

Then one day after dinner, I asked Fortune about the letter. She simply snatched it from me and walked out, and then she came back one hour later, and took the baby from me. She was off from work that evening, so after she had given the baby a bath and put her to bed, I asked her about the letter again. Then she snapped, "Why did you read my letter?"

I suspect you'd expect me to shout, curse, throw my fist, or break something. But I did not do any of that nature; instead, I remembered the pledge I made to her few minutes before departing Nigeria. So I collected my thoughts and began to plan immediately in my mind to send her to Nigeria to bring the baby to the United States to be with his mother—only if she would say, "Yes, I had a baby in Nigeria before coming over." She could have added, "It's not your business," and it would not have mattered because I realized that millions of people adopt other people's children and raise them like their own biological children. Admittedly, I would have been happy to assume the part of the baby's father. However, this was the caveat: I was not willing to exercise that goodwill unless she first talked to me about the baby.

On April 20, 1980, my second daughter, Ugo, arrived full term, a fat, plump baby. Like her sister Ere, when I picked her up in the hospital, she startled a bit and managed to open her eyes. "Yes, it's Daddy," I said and kissed her forehead. Meanwhile, I continued to beg Fortune to talk about her son, but she refused and said, "When the time comes."

On September 4, 1985, my third and youngest daughter, Chika, arrived. And then we moved to a three-family rental property we bought in Brockton, Massachusetts. As with her two sisters, the first time the nurse handed her over to me in the hospital, she opened her eyes and smiled after startling a little. Although I did not know what those baby-signs meant. However, I felt like I had a little angel in my hands each time.

In any case, the birth of my children did not solve my marriage problem, so then I began to kneel down and beg at midnight, midday, six o'clock in the morning, and six o'clock in the evening.

Still, Fortune continued to insist that she would talk about the baby only when the time came. Therefore, I began to wonder what time she was talking about and why she could say, "when the time comes," but unable to utter one word: "Yes."

Then I began to feel the effect of her mental abuse until the frowny look on my face turned into wrinkles.

When I was a student at GTC Enugu, I had attended the Fourth of July celebration at the American consulate and fell in love with America after reading the preamble to the American Declaration of Independence:

"We hold these truths to be self-evident, that all men are created equal, that they are endowed, by their Creator, with certain unalienable Rights, that among these are Life, Liberty, and the pursuit of Happiness."

What struck me the most and I had cherished was the word "liberty" in particular. Like life itself, I see it as the basis upon which relationship decisions ought to be made. So I prayed that Fortune would allow me to enjoy the liberty to foreclose the matter and save my marriage. Therefore, I tried one more time. "Please, Fortune, please talk to me about that baby. Please just say yes," I said.

"I said when the time comes," she said.

Then I knelt down, held her hands, and said, "I hate to say these words:

That time will never come for me; consider this marriage over because you have denied me the liberty to exercise rare goodwill most men would not extend to their wives in a situation like this.

In short, that was the moment I separated from Fortune, ended my marriage, severed my relationship with her, and moved my personal belongings to the guest room without yelling or cursing. No, you did not hear any foul language flying around, and the children did not know what had happened.

In a way, I was happy that we had had three children at that moment because when Fortune and I were in love and just dating, we

A MATTER OF FAITH

had planned to have three children if we were fertile. At least we accomplished one goal together.

For the most part, though, taking care my children, watching them crash in and out of the door with their friends to drink some juice and run out again, made my life after work so worthwhile.

Running bath water, giving them baths, sitting around after dinner to talk about school, and set goals gave me a sense of assurance that they would be OK.

Dropping them off at school, and watching them wave back and run to class made me feel as if they were on the right track to appreciating school and wanting to learn.

And teaching them how to deal with bullies at school; rules at home, and deciding together who got what kind of punishment for minor infractions after dinner, made us seem like a functioning family.

So there we were still happy, even the troublemakers whom I spanked with a soft flat paper paddle or with my finger as a disciplinary measure.

One day in 1990, on a blistering summer day, when I was on my way home from work, Chika ran out to me as I was parking my car.

"Daddy," she said sobbing. "You won't believe what happened today."

"What happened, sweetheart?" I asked.

"People in long white gowns and long beards came to our house," she said. "They lit candles and incense everywhere; they sang and danced; they sprinkled water and powder everywhere in our house, and they said that they were driving an evil spirit away. Daddy, do you know who the evil spirit is?"

"No, sweetheart, what did they say?" I asked.

"Daddy, they said that you are the evil spirit," she said and broke out crying.

"So, what do you think?" I asked.

"You are not the evil spirit," she said. "You are the best daddy in the whole world."

"Stop crying," I said. "The most important thing is what you think. Come on, let's have some ice cream."

While we were still eating the ice cream, Fortune walked in and told the kids about a revival they were having at the church and made me aware for the first time that she was involved with the cult—Cherubim and Seraphim, founded in Nigeria.

On Sunday, the day of the revival, I went to church with my children, and their mother, just to ease the worries in Chika's mind about her father being an evil spirit. When the revival started, the priest announced the names of the very special invitees—seven to be exact and among them was my name.

The pulpit was transformed into a shaded altar from which dark-bluish smoke poured out and filled the church. With candles lit all around, and the smell of powder and incense mixed in the air to produce an atmosphere of magic and serenity, I experienced the occult festival for the first time.

When the celebration got underway, people came out in front of the congregation and confessed their transgressions, and the high priest admonished the transgressors.

Next, the prophets and the prophetesses lined up and the special invitees behind them, we danced around the church through the aisles. Suddenly, one prophet announced the names of people who would come into wealth in the future, and then they donated money to the church. Another prophetess declared the names of people who would win the lottery in the future, and they too came out and made donations. The second priest in the ranks conducted a free-for-all prayer, during which people yelled and prayed loudly; some staggered and fell, and the priest prayed for them.

The highlight came when the high priest came out in, amazingly decorated red-gold=and-white gown, surrounded by the priests and the prophets. The dark smoke poured out of the altar and filled the church, deafening music began to play as he stood in front of the congregation and announced the names of the people he said should change their evil ways. I was not sure whether those people he called out were even in the church. Regardless the music began to play again. The special invitees lined up behind the prophets as the prophetesses trailed, and then we danced around and around the church. And then the high priest said the closing prayer.

A MATTER OF FAITH

As I turned and looked at my children. Chika seemed petrified, from the look on her face. Then the whole congregation rose and joined in the dance, and the occasion ended.

Before we left the church, one of the priests escorted my family and me to the parking lot and said, "We are glad you could come today, I look forward to seeing you every Sunday." Then I replied, "I came to hear you call me an evil spirit as you did in my absence, in my house, and in front of my children."

"Oh, I thought you came to worship with us," he said and left.

"Yeah, why didn't the big priest tell Daddy that he's an evil spirit?" Chika asked.

"His spirit is too strong," their mother answered.

"Daddy, I was scared when I saw you are dancing behind the big priest," Chika said.

"Are you happy now?" I asked her.

"Yes, Daddy, I am. I hate those priests," she said.

"Chika! You should not say that" Ugo warned her.

I had bought my second house at 27 Pleasant Street, Brockton, Massachusetts, the next street down from the first. Shortly after, Fortune moved to a two-bedroom apartment, and then I rented all six apartments in the two properties to tenants with Section 8 government housing assistance.

In chapter 6, I recalled the trip I made to Nigeria to have my immigrant visa processed. Well, during that trip, I filed for expedited divorce because I had a civil marriage in Nigeria. So before returning to the United States, the court granted me a divorce, but I did not give Fortune her copy of the divorce decree when I came back.

Then after I had gotten a job in Chicago and told my children, and heard Fortune say that the kids would not go anywhere with me, I felt it was time to give her the divorce decree.

In some ways, her decision not to move to Chicago with me was just as well because our marriage had ended and I was looking for a simple reason my children would understand to give her the divorce decree.

The two properties we owned were grossing three thousand-two hundred-twenty-two dollars per month in rent money. So to make sure Fortune had full financial control of the rental properties, I introduced her to the Housing and Urban Development (HUD) office and put all the renters on direct deposit.

Before I left for Chicago, I gave Fortune copies of the deeds for the two houses, the real-estate-account checkbook, and my personal-account checkbook because I had made it a joint account. Then I introduced her to my attorney in case she needed legal help.

Finally, I gave her my divorce decree and left after hugging my children.

I believed that by doing all these things, I had set her up pretty well for life, and she would not have any problem taking care of the needs of our children. Above all, for me, it was a clean break.

***

Shortly after I arrived in Chicago, my friends in Boston began to calls to tell me that Fortune was spreading rumors that she did not move to Chicago with me because I was trying to kill her.

In 1993, three years after I had left Brockton, Fortune left our minor children alone and traveled to Nigeria. Once when I did my nightly call to my children, Chika told me, "Daddy, Mommy left us alone and went to Nigeria. Please, Daddy, don't tell anybody."

It was apparent that her action was child neglect and abuse—serious enough for me to pursue custody. However, I would never dream of separating my children from their mother.

Additionally, I recalled in chapter 8, the events that happened when my children visited me in Minnesota with their mother. Well, after that visit she moved from Brockton to Florida to live and hid the children from me for three years.

Again there is no doubt that her action was clearly a case of abduction and kidnapping, which were severe enough to land her in jail if I had chosen to hurt her. Still, I never did anything to hurt her. So I agonized for years; still believing that God would lead me to my children. Indeed, I had left it as a matter of faith.

A MATTER OF FAITH

One weekend, I went to Boston without aforethought, and no idea why I was making the trip. But when I arrived in Boston, I decided to visit an old friend, Dr. Everett Onuoha. I arrived at his house and found the door locked, and nobody answered the doorbell. Then as I turned around to leave, his wife, Ester, got out of her car in the parking lot and yelled, "Mr. Ndukwe, stop." I stopped, turned around, and saw Ester running toward me. "I am just coming back from Florida," she said. "I spent some time with your kids. Come inside; let me call them. I want you to talk to those kids."

Then she called them up.

"Hello, Ugo, hold on," she said and gave me the phone.

"Ugo, this is Daddy. How are you?" I inquired.

Ugo kept quiet for a while; then she hung the phone up.

"Don't worry. I have Fortune's number and address. What Fortune is doing to those kids is shameful," Ester said.

At that moment, my emotions became overwhelming by because I had predicted that God would lead me to where my kids were without going anywhere to search for them. But I never knew it would happen this way.

"Thank you so much, Ester," I said.

"You are welcome," she said. "I am sorry I can't offer you anything because I am just returning from my vacation."

"Where is Dr. Onuoha?" I asked.

"It has been years since we got divorced," she said. "But our kids are with him because they have nothing to do with our problems."

"I can't believe it. What happened?" I asked. "I know that you did not join your husband with any baggage, as my ex did."

"Our marriage just went downhill until I couldn't take it anymore," she said.

"Oh dear, I am so sorry," I said.

"It's OK. Here is Onuoha's address. The kids are there," she said. "Go and see him. The kids would love to see their favorite uncle, Chuks."

Now high from the information about my children, I stopped briefly at Dr. Onuoha's, and he received me warmly. Then we chatted for a while before I returned to New Jersey.

A week later, when I called my kids in Florida, Chika picked up the phone and said, "Hello, who is this?"

"Chika, how are you?" I inquired.

As I expected, she kept quiet for a while and hung the phone up. It was a slow start to our eventual reunion. Now four weeks had passed since I made contact with my children, and I had had time to think about the immense pain they might have been feeling.

I remembered my childhood—how lost, empty, and hopeless I felt each time either of my parents stayed out later than my brother and I expected. I thought about how intensely angry I felt and how nobody and nothing could calm me down except the sight of my father and mom's sweet voice. I remembered accusing my parents of not thinking about me and my brother and how it did not matter whether or not they had good reasons for staying out late; I simply warned them not to stay out late again. So I decided to go to Florida and see my children.

On Labor Day 1999, I traveled to Maryland with my girlfriend, Renee and arrived at my cousin Onwuchekwa's house early in the evening. Then after dinner, I told him that I would be going to Florida alone and my girlfriend would stay with them while I was gone.

"No, Uncle, I will not let you drive to Florida alone," he said. "It's too far. I'll go with you and share the driving."

So we left Maryland very early in the morning to beat the traffic and arrived in Tampa late at night.

The following day, my children visited me at the hotel I was staying.

"I am sorry that you have to experience the unimaginable," I said. "I wish things were different. But you can count on my abiding and unconditional love."

"Mommy told me that you did not want me when I was born. Why?" Chika asked.

"Do you believe it?" I asked her. "How can you forget how happy I used to be playing with you?"

"Why didn't you come and look for us?" Ugo asked.

A MATTER OF FAITH

"I did not know where you were until Ester told me," I said.

"Why did you abandon us?" Ere asked.

"First, your mother had a son with another man," I said. "Then, when I asked her about it, she insulted me by refusing to talk to me about the baby for five years. Second, she refused to go to Chicago with me. No, I did not abandon you. She kept you away from me."

"Yes, her son is here now, and she says that he is our brother. No, he is not. It is all her fault. I hate her," Ere said.

"Yes, it's her fault," Chika and Ugo agreed.

I intervened instinctively to defend their mother. And said, "Please stop. I am not here to talk about your mother. I am here to reunite with you. So can we promise not to separate again?"

"Look at what she's done," Ugo went on...

"Let's stop blaming your mother," I said again. "She's not a bad woman."

Later that evening, I took them out to their favorite restaurant and began to chat.

"Chika, you are graduating from high school. Have you decided on which college you want to attend?" I asked.

"She is going to UMass," Fortune interrupted.

"Mommy wants me to go there," Chika said.

I stopped talking because I was close to exploding with anger for having Fortune interrupt our conversation.

Ugo was working for Time Warner and attending college part-time, and her job was paying her tuition fees. By then, Ere was in the military. So I said to Ugo, "Ugo, what do you want from Daddy?"

"Daddy, I want a Honda," she said.

"OK, can you direct me to the dealership?" I asked.

When we got to the Honda dealership, I bought a Honda Accord for her. Then I turned to Ere and said, "What do you want, Ere?"

"Why did you not give Mommy any child support? Why didn't you?" she asked angrily.

"To begin with, I was sending her four hundred dollars every two weeks when I got paid, until she left Brockton," I said. "Also I left our two houses for her, plus my bank account and our real estate bank account. Public records showed that she collected over seventy-six thousand dollars in rent money in three years without paying mortgages and taxes. The IRS even garnished my salary for that, and I had to file for bankruptcy because of her actions. I don't want to hear about child support."

"Where did I keep the money?" their mother interjected. "I used the money to fix the houses."

The following day, Onwuchekwa and I returned to Maryland. Then Renee and I returned to New Jersey the next morning.

Finally, the long-awaited reunion with my children happened in the summer of 2000 when I sent plane tickets to Ugo and Chika. The day they arrived in Newark, I waited at the baggage claim, as they had requested. And immediately they saw me, they jumped on me, and all of us fell to the ground—indeed It was daughter-father passion built up over the years of separation. "I wanted a hug, not a wrestling match," I said.

I must admit that spontaneous outburst of emotion and public expression of affection, has stayed fresh in my mind.

Chapter 12
Defrauded

Let no man go beyond or defraud his brother, for, though it be hidden from man, it will be found that God is the avenger of all such.

~ Matthew Henry

Generally speaking, everything was going spectacularly well for me in 1999. I had the job of a research and development manager at a prestigious company, and I was content with my salary. So I sent an F1 visa-application package to my nephew. Emmanuel, in Ghana—after a series of consultations with the US Immigration and Naturalization Services' personnel in Newark, New Jersey.

As summer was winding down, I received a letter from him to inform me that he had obtained the visa and his arrival date. Then on the day of his arrival, I went to JFK International Airport in New York with my girlfriend, Renee, to wait for him. Suddenly, I looked at the monitor and found that his plane had landed. I had forgotten that he had to go through immigration processing, so I panicked and began to look for him. I checked the line of people getting into taxis without a trace of him, so I decided to go back inside the terminal to search again and finally I saw him coming out. We hugged and got in the car and returned home. A few weeks later, I escorted him to Union County College and registered him for classes.

One day, during a phone conversation with my cousin Onwuchekwa Okoro, we discussed my worries about my nephew. During that call, he gave me an endless list of young men from Nigeria who had come over to the United States and gotten into trouble. I knew some of the boys he talked about. Thinking that he's not like those other characters, we called each other every other day; sometimes we spent hours on the phone, talking about things I never knew about Nigerians. Gradually I began to trust him to the extent of relying on him on matters relating to our village and Nigeria. When he visited me, we had a cordial discussion. Similarly, when I visited him, he was generous and treated me respectfully.

With all these in mind plus the fact that he drove to Florida without me asking him to go with me on that day I reunited with my children, I felt comfortable trusting him.

One day, we spent hours talking about what I could do to prevent Emmanuel from getting into trouble. So he suggested that I send Emmanuel to Ghana.

"That will not help," I said.

With the knowledge of where my office was located, Onwuchekwa came to my office once. We spent some time together and had lunch at the cafeteria. At that lunch, we talked quite a bit about Emmanuel. I remember him saying, "Uncle, I have figured out what will be ideal for Emmanuel."

"What is it?" I asked.

"I own a franchise called Pack and Post Plus," he said. "It is like Mail Boxes Etc. If you buy one, I will train Emmanuel, and he can manage it during summer holidays and weekends. That will keep him out of trouble."

Of all the ideas we talked about, that was the best yet, so immediately, without a second thought, I bought the idea.

"How much does it cost?" I asked.

"Mail Boxes Etc. Costs a hundred fifty-six thousand dollars, but I bought a Pack and Post Plus for a hundred twenty-five thousand dollars. We have to see if they are doing promotions," he said.

"I can't afford that," I said.

"The business pays for itself," he said. "I have already recouped what I paid for mine."

Then after lunch, we chatted some more in my office where he said,

A MATTER OF FAITH

"The business is so good that my wife and I work in the store during the morning hours owing to heavy store traffic, she takes boxes of express and priority mails to the post office in the afternoon. Then she goes home from there, and then I manage the store by myself until closing. I will come to New Jersey and train Emmanuel and anybody else you hire to run the store for you."

"How about sending Emmanuel to Maryland to work with you during summer so he can acquire on-the-job training?"

"That will work as well," he said, "the down payment is seventy-nine thousand. If you give me a check made out to Pack and Post Plus, I will forward it with a strong recommendation because I am a franchisee in good standing."

Blinded to the intrigue of a Nigerian scam-artist, I wrote a check-in that amount and gave it to him before he left. One week later, he sent me an e-mail to confirm that my application had been approved pending payment of the balance of forty-six thousand dollars. Then I replied and informed him that I could send him thirty-nine thousand dollars right then and the balance in a few weeks. A few minutes later, he called me.

"OK, I can add seven thousand dollars of my own, and you can pay me back whenever you can," he said.

After giving my cousin a hundred twenty-five thousand dollars to pay for my franchise, I thought that I had completed the deal. Instead, I received an e-mail asking me to wire eighteen thousand dollars for the equipment I needed to run the business. Then I called Onwuchekwa up and said, "I received an e-mail from pack and post plus asking for eighteen thousand dollars for equipment. What is that all about?" I inquired.

"Uncle, that's cheap," he said. "I paid twenty thousand dollars. The money is for your color printer, computer, fax machine, packaging supplies, mailbox system, credit card scanner, and all brands of cell phones."

Still oblivious to the trickery of the scam-artist, I wired the money to the account number provided in the e-mail. Then Onwuchekwa visited me a couple of times, and both of us drove around New Jersey, to look for a demographically appropriate location for the store.

Finally, we chose a shopping strip—Talmadge, in Edison, New Jersey where I found a vacant store for rent, signed the lease, and spent a significant amount of money to get the store ready for business. Then I waited for the equipment that I had paid for until I ran out of patience and called Onwuchekwa and said, "Can you believe that I haven't received my equipment from Pack and Post Plus?"

"Uncle, their operations manager was on vacation, I will check to see when he is returning to work," he said.

As summer, arrived and colleges were on break, I sent Emmanuel to Maryland to learn how to run the business. Now, I worked on the store on weekends and got it ready for the grand opening. The neon signage was completed and lit up, promotional banners hung around the shopping strip, and I prepared for my cousin to start training somebody to run the store.

Then one Monday, Onwuchekwa called me and said, "Uncle, I am checking the list of the equipment Pack and Post Plus sent to you, and your color-copy machine is not on the list, I will find out why."

"Can you get on the phone and call them right now?" I asked angrily.

"I will call you right back," he said.

He called back a few minutes later and said, "Uncle, your color-copy machine was shipped two days ago, I will rent a truck and bring everything over on Saturday."

"OK, one more week of waiting won't hurt," I said.

While waiting for my store equipment, I called Onwuchekwa to discuss the grand opening events, but he did not answer, so I called a few more times and got the answering machine. A few days later, I called Onwuchekwa again. That time, that annoying number-disconnected message greeted me. Therefore, I called his house.

"Hello, who is this?" his son asked.

"Junior, this is Uncle Chuks. Can I speak to your daddy?" I asked.

"My daddy is gone, but mommy is here," he said.

"Give Mommy the phone," I said.

"Mommy, it's Uncle Chuks," he said.

"Hi, Uncle Chuks, how are you?" she greeted.

"Where is your husband?" I asked.

A MATTER OF FAITH

"He traveled to Nigeria last week," she said. "He planned to travel to Geneva, in Switzerland from Nigeria. I haven't heard from him."

"OK, thank you," I said.

"Uncle, do you have any message for him in case he calls?" she asked.

"No, I don't have any message," I said.

After hanging up the phone, I realized that I had been had. I had heard of schemes Nigerians had been using to defraud people, called 419 scams, but I never thought I would be so naïve as to fall victim. I was enraged, shocked, and helpless because I had spent my life savings on the business—that was a scam. Still hoping for a piece of better news, I called his house a couple of times, and his wife told me he had not called her from Nigeria.

Nevertheless, I opened the store as a cell-phone retail store. I used the money I had left at the time to buy phones from AT&T, Nextel, Verizon, and T-Mobile on a cash-on-delivery basis.

My first week at the business was not as bad as I had expected since I sold a few plans, enough to pay the rent, but the billing cycle was so long that by the time I got paid by the service providers, my store was empty, so I could not continue.

Speaking of the devil, I received a call from Onwuchekwa's wife begging, "Uncle, I have been trying to reach Ike, and I don't know where he is. I've been served an eviction notice, and I don't know where to go with the kids. I need your help."

"Well, things aren't going well with me," I said, "I am sorry I can't help you."

"Please, Uncle, please help us. I will give the money back to you when he comes back. I promise," she said.

As she was talking, her baby girl began to cry, forcing me to act against my will. Sure—babies' voices always make my heart soft, so I asked, "How much is your rent?"

"Uncle, it is two thousand seven hundred thirty-five dollars. That's how much we are renting this house for," she said.

"Ifechi, I would not like to have to call you for my money. Are you sure you will pay me back?" I asked.

"Yes, Uncle, trust me," she said.

So I sent her a check for two thousand seven hundred thirty-five dollars by overnight mail.

Meanwhile, I began thinking of how to pursue her husband for perpetrating such a scam on me. So I went to the district attorney's office in Linden, New Jersey, and sought his advice. After reviewing the document I gave him, he went to another office, as I sat there in his office and waited until he came back.

"This is a federal crime because it involves a money transfer across the state lines," he said.

Then he advised me to write down everything I knew about the case and forward it to the FBI. "You'll be required to back up every claim with evidence," he said.

"Are you suggesting that I hire an attorney to write a legal brief?" I inquired.

"No, just a chronological account of all the transactions," he said.

On the district attorney's advice, I went home and compiled a day-by-day account of the transactions, and called the number he had given me. Then the person who answered the phone said, "this kind of case is better handled by the postal inspector's office. Send it to the Newark office. Their investigator will review your claims."

A few weeks after I had sent the document to the postal inspector's office in Newark, New Jersey, I got a call from the inspector's office saying.

"We've received your account of the crime committed against you, and we are actively reviewing it," he said. "Your case is within the jurisdiction of this office, so we will be advising you on the matter."

Surprisingly, Ifechi called me up one day and said, "Uncle, Ike came back, but he's gone again, I mailed you a check yesterday. Thank you for helping me."

Sure, she sent me the check, but when I deposited it in my bank account, it bounced due to insufficient funds. But when I called Ifechi that annoying message—the-number-you-called-has-been-disconnected came on to assure me that the grand scam-plus was complete.

A MATTER OF FAITH

My unemployment benefits had run out, and I had not been to the bank in a while. Therefore, I went to the bank in downtown Linden, New Jersey, to check on my account balance.

"The account had been closed," the cashier told me.

"I never closed the account," I responded. "In fact, I had some balance in the account last time I made a withdrawal. Who closed it?"

"From what I can see, the account was closed automatically for inactivity," the cashier said.

I came out of the bank as people pound the pavement with an air of normalcy and permanence while in my reality; the world was crumbling beneath me. They seemed to breathe in and out regularly and freely while I was suffocating and sinking fast into an abyss of despair and hopelessness—hardly breathing. I roamed around for a while without feeling the ground I walked on. The day hung around longer than usual, the sun refused to set; nature denied me sympathy, and sleep seemed elusive.

A few days later, I got a call from my brother-in-law, Babatunde Adewunmi saying, "Uncle, I have been laid off too, this economy is getting worse."

"Oh my God, what are we going to do? My situation is bad enough," I said. "But you are with your family. That adds a different dimension to our problem. Have you written your résumé?"

"Don't worry, Uncle," he said. "I am going to start my own business and make money with my pen and pencil."

Tunde started an engineering company and called me up to work with him every now and then, and he paid me for my time. I had received an eviction notice, so I moved my belongings to storage space and moved in with my girlfriend in Newark, New Jersey, similarly, my nephew moved in with his friends.

On my last day in Linden, I received a check for three hundred dollars from my niece Comfort with a note, "Chuks, I feel terrible for what happened to you, I hope these few dollars will help."

Immediately that check lifted my flagging spirit out of the rubbles of financial disaster and sent me on a mental walk to a sacred place in my mind where I make vital decisions. So after a few minutes of deliberation—it was a no-brainer, I decided that I would not cash the check; instead, I saved it in my trunk.

Some readers may find my action weird, and others may find it senseless. I agree with all that. Still, there are times when principle and value collide and compel us to do things or behave in ways that seem weird or strange such as in the situation I found myself.

It was not until that moment that I realized why I always declined to say how much I was worth during job interviews. As it turned out, it was a principle I did not know I had—not to associate human values with money.

In this case, my niece's action was worth more than money to me. I still look at her check sometimes and feel satisfied that one of the people I cherish in my life cares about me to the extent of giving me the money and I preserved my principle and treasured the gift.

My brother-in-law's new business was beginning to take shape, and my worries about him and his wife, my niece Grace, had substantially diminished. We called each other occasionally just to see how things were going. One day, he called me and asked, "Uncle, are you working today?"

"No, I am home," I replied.

"A couple of jobs came up," he said. "You can go with me if you want."

"Sure, I would like to go with you," I said.

So we drove to Plainfield and passed our destination. We ran around the block a couple of times and found the address; then we began to take measurements. I held one end of the tape while he rolled out the tape and recorded the lengths. Occasionally he would tell me where to start and stop. It went something like this:

"Uncle, we will measure from the end of the street. Go down; some more, keep going; a little bit; I will tell you when to stop; right there."

When we finished the job, we went to Edison Industrial Park to look for some equipment he needed for his business. However, I cannot remember whether he bought the instrument, leased it, or ordered one.

Anyways, we left Edison and went to West New York for another job. Getting there, Tunde told the man who sat at the porch that "we were there to survey the plot,"

A MATTER OF FAITH

As we began to survey the plot, a sweet aroma began to permeate the air and made me feel as if I had to have whatever it was, but I had no money to buy it. Then I looked around and saw smoke rising from one chimney, and clouding the neighborhood. Tunde must have noticed me looking in that direction because he said, "Uncle, that's the smell of freshly baked bread. It is making me hungry, too, we will get some when we finish."

In less than three hours, we completed the job, and then we packed up our tools and went to the bakery. There Tunde picked the loaves he liked and asked, "Uncle, which ones do you want?"

"I don't have any money," I answered.

"Don't worry. I will pay for it," Tunde said.

When we got to his house, my niece had cooked rice, so we ate and watched TV for a while and then Tunde paid me for the day and said, "Uncle, whenever you are not busy, give me a call and see whether I have a job for us to do."

A few weeks later, while Tunde and I were at work in East Orange, New Jersey, he told me of a man who was selling his van. "his son went to college with Chijioke and Eke," he said and gave me the man's telephone number.

In the chapter titled "Helping Hands," I wrote in detail how I became the new owner of the van without paying a dime for it. Two days after the mechanic who repaired the van handed it over to me, a company called Priority located in the industrial park in Edison, New Jersey hired me. So I worked for the company delivering pharmaceutical products to nursing and private homes and later delivering auto parts for Toyota of Morristown.

In any event, I made money with the van but spent every penny I made to repair it.

Chapter 13
Helping Hands

To give pleasure to a single heart by a single act is better than a thousand heads bowing in prayer.

~ Mahatma Gandhi

I recalled in chapter 1, the first time I became the beneficiary of American generosity. I had arrived in the US a few months earlier: the only black person in the neighborhood, and a stranger for that matter. So each time I came outside to play with the kids, to go to school, or work dogs would line up on both sides of the street, bark, and chase after me as residents watched until I went out of their sight.

Consequently, when an old lady, Miss Wendy's generous heart could not take any more of the dogs chasing me up and down the blocks of 11 College road in Burlington, Massachusetts; she gave me a brand-new Toyota Corolla to keep the dogs aware from me.

My second experience came in 1985 when I escorted a Codex coworker, Larry J. to inspect a house he wanted to buy in Brockton, Massachusetts.

The realtor was not in the office when we arrived, so we sat in his lobby to wait for him and discussed the problems I had been having with my project. I looked outside and saw a man limping rather severely and trying to crawl up the steps. So I rushed out of the office and helped the man—a white man—to get up the steps. He was not a small man, by any means. I remember his right hand around my neck as I held it with my right hand and my left hand around his waist as we climbed the steps one at a time. Then I surrendered my seat to him and said, "Sir, the realtor is not in the office, have a seat. We are all waiting for him."

"I'm the realtor," he replied.

I had no idea—what I had done counted for a good deed. Anyways, I opened the office door, and then Mr. Schumer went inside his office.

A MATTER OF FAITH

Soon he came out and gave a couple who had sat beside Larry a check. And surprisingly the couple walked out without a thank-you. Then he talked to another couple before taking Larry and me to the house Larry had come to inspect.

"What do you think?" he asked Larry.

"Beautiful," Larry answered. "But I have to bring my wife to see it before we continue."

"I will hold it for you if you put something down on it," the realtor said.

"I would love to, but I don't have my checkbook with me, and I don't have any money on me either. I will come back."

✸✸✸

Before we left the realtor's office, he gave me his business card at the back of which he wrote, "Helped up the steps" while Larry was in the bathroom, and asked me to come back alone and see him.

So I went back to the realtor's office the next day and knocked on his door.

"Come in young man," he said. "Can I help you?"

Then I gave him the card he had given me the previous day.

"Oh yes, have a seat," he said.

At that moment, the realtor, Mr. Schumer—I gleaned from the card he had given me—gave me a short sermon on good deeds, empathy, and humanity—and the reward of treating others as oneself.

"Do you own a house, or just renting an apartment?" he asked.

"I'm renting an apartment," I answered.

Then he told me about his first house on Wilmington Street and said, "I have made lots of money since then."

Also, he told me about the couple he had given a check to the previous day and said, "that couple was my daughter and her boyfriend. They come here, they sit around the house, and they watch me struggle to get in the office and in my house without getting up to help me."

"And there you were—a total stranger, the first time you saw me, you ran forward to help me. Do you realize you could have tripped and broken your hands, legs, neck, or something else?"

He offered me a cup of coffee and continued preaching. "Good people don't know they are good, and they don't know when they've done a good deed. That is what makes this world a wonderful place worth living in. You're a good man. Let me show you a house. If you like it, it's yours."

"I just got out of college. I can't afford a house yet," I said.

"Let's look at it first, OK?"

Then he drove to 25 Wilmington Street and sat down. Construction workers were remodeling the house, erecting the steps for the patio, a gate for the driveway, and the back door.

"Take your time and go from the basement to the third floor," he said. "All the doors are open. Take a good look and tell me what you think of the house."

"I like the house," I said after the grand tour.

"The only thing left is the boiler, and that baby is ready to go," he said.

Still, I was not ready to even begin to think of buying a house. Then he gave me a tutorial on buying and owning a home in the United States. More so than his persuasive tutorial and encouragement, he gave me a check for seven thousand dollars to deposit in my bank account.

"Open a separate real-estate account with this check, and keep adding money in it," he said. "The mortgage bank will track that account for six months. That's the law."

Next, Mr. Schumer began to draft a bank offer-to-buy letter and demanded my name, address, place of work, salary, and date of birth. When he finished the letter, he showed me what the bank offer letter looked like.

"If the bank approves this letter," he said, "that baby is yours, but you will write a check for me in the same amount as your down payment for the house. Call me in two weeks."

So two weeks later, I called Mr. Schumer back to ask about the offer letter.

A MATTER OF FAITH

"The loan was approved," he said. "We'll wait for the bank to schedule your closing date, and then you'll write me a check for seven thousand dollars as your down payment. Congratulations."

Admittedly, I had heard the saying "every good deed deserves another" but I never imagined that I'd do anything that good to deserve buying a house with zero down payment.

Spurred on by Mr. Schumer's generous gesture, which thrust me into the real estate world, I went on to buy another house, at 27 Pleasant Street, the next street down from my first also from Mr. Schumer—two years later.

My last experience began when my brother-in-law, Tunde, and I were doing a survey in East Orange and chatting about the courier business. While I was describing the industry, I said, "It seems as if you can't make any money working for the courier company unless you have a cargo van."

"There's a man in Westfield who is selling his van," Tunde said. "His son went to school with Chijioke and Eke. I will get his number, and have you ask him about the van."

"That would be good," I said.

So the next time I went to work with Tunde, he gave me the man's number, then I called him up when I got home and said, "Mr. Fernandez, my name is Chuks, I am looking for a van to buy, and I would like to come and look at the van you have for sale."

"Yes, the van is here. It is a Ford Econo Two-Fifty, with two hundred twenty thousand miles on it, well maintained," he said.

"When can I look at it?" I asked.

"How about tomorrow after three o'clock?" he asked.

"Sounds like a plan. Give me directions to your house," I said.

When I arrived at his house the following day, I parked in front of his house.

"Mr. Fernandez, my name is Chuks. I spoke to you yesterday about the van," I said.

As I was talking, he bent over, looked inside my car in which I had packages, envelopes, and delivery confirmation slips all over the back seat.

"Are you doing a delivery job with a Lexus?" he asked.

"Yes, sir, I have no choice," I said and told him what had happened to me and forced me to take on the job of freelance messenger services.

"Good Lord, that's terrible," he said. "Come inside the house. What would you like to drink?"

"That will be Pepsi-Cola," I said.

Then he popped a can of Pepsi and gave it to me as we chatted about my professional career and the scam that brought me to the state of bankruptcy.

"I am so sorry for what happened to you," he said. "I used this van for my business, so I maintained it real good. But it has a problem with the radiator so I will tow it to my mechanic's shop in Elizabeth, and you can pick it up there when the radiator is fixed. You don't have to worry about the cost; I will pay the mechanic for the repair."

"Sir, you haven't told me how much you are asking for it yet," I said.

"I am not asking you for a penny. I want you to park that Lexus and use the van for your job," he said.

Then he gave me the key for the van and the certificate of title. And as I was leaving his house, he stopped me and said, "I have to put down an amount on the title; otherwise you won't be able to register it with the Department of Motor Vehicles."

So he wrote down twenty-five dollars as the purchase price on the title. When I got home, I called Tunde and told him about the van.

"That's great, Uncle. Now you can make some money with the van," Tunde said.

Three days later, I called the mechanic to check on the van.

"This is Mario. Can I help you?" he asked.

"Mario, my name is Chuks. Mr. Fernandez towed a van to your shop," I said. "Have you fixed the radiator yet?"

"Yes, it is done. You can pick it up anytime," Mr. Fernandez said.

Finally, I took a bus to his shop and picked up the van, and it was in pretty good shape.

Simply stated and in my humble and appreciative estimation, I have had my share of American generosity, and I am thankful.

Chapter 14
Faith And Courage

You're not alone, and you're not the one in charge," Mother said gently. "Ask for help when you need it, and give help when you can. I think that is how we serve God—and each other and ourselves—in times as dark as these.

~ Kristin Hannah

It is not the asking but the courage to ask and the faith that what you are asking for; you will receive. That's how I see the synergy between courage and faith whenever I ask God for help—to me, that's the miracle of faith. But I did not suspect that one day, my smart-ass viewpoint on this philosophical thinking would be severely tested. And then it happened.

Aside from not making money delivering auto parts as a freelance messenger, my van had been in the repair shop for four weeks for a broken rear axle that would cost lots of money to fix. So I did not make any money in four weeks. In other words, I was unemployed and broke—so damn broke! It was shameful.

In the early morning hours of that summer day in 2007, my clock alarm went off—although I had nowhere to go, it was just a bad habit of mine. I turned over in my bed and kicked the alarm clock off the nightstand. The sun was already out, and the light was peeping through my faux-wood horizontal blinds. What's a man who has nowhere to go do? So I curled up and covered myself, then the alarm went off again, and so I got up feeling weird.

For no apparent reason, I began to think about the times I was still living with my family, a wife and three daughters; the time I was a manager at Lucent Technologies, designing Internet gateways; and how good life was when I had two houses, a good job, and money.

Chuks I, Ndukwe

Suddenly I was gripped by that eerie disabling fear—the kind you feel when thick dark clouds cover the sky, high winds force trees to dance to a breaking point, houses shake, and debris hits doors, windows, and roofs with rocket-like sounds.

However, when I opened the window, everything was normal as a gentle breeze caressed those who were up and about their business.

Then after breakfast, I went out to look for a day job—manual labor to ensure that I had some money in my pocket and to escape the boredom from staying idle at home.

For the most part, my life had been reduced to sitting around, waiting for my van to be fixed—wondering how I'd pay for the repair and whether I would ever find an engineering job again after failing for six years. By my account, delivering auto parts and pharmaceutical products and making no money did not qualify as employment.

Outright broke and unemployed, and having lost everything I owned when the franchise I bought turned out to be a scam, I had a little to look forward to. Still, I persevered and sought comfort in my faith.

On my way home that evening, I stopped by the gas station by my apartment building to buy a pack of peanut. With my wallet open and one hand inside my pocket, I had no money on me—not a single dollar in my wallet nor a penny in my pocket to pay for the peanut. So I put the pack of peanut back on the rack.

When I got home, I checked my pantry not to pick-out something to cook but to remind myself that I had nothing to prepare. Then I searched the entire apartment, looking for some money I might have misplaced carelessly and found nothing.

Additionally, I checked all my pants again—unfolding each pocket inside out and not even a penny dropped out of any pocket.

It was Friday evening, which made no difference since every day had become a weekend for me. At that moment, there was nothing I could do but to lay down and stare at the ceiling.

Yes, I was hungry but had no appetite to eat. Moreover, my head has heated to a boiling point. And was about to explode. And above all, I had prayed and looked for a job since I was laid off from my job— engineering manager at Lucent Technologies, in New Jersey, in 2001— six years prior.

A MATTER OF FAITH

Worst yet, at that moment, I had an eviction notice in my hand. And hours from knocking at the door of a homeless shelter to ask for a bed.

So I became irate and not in the mood for praying. Why? You may ask. Because all my life, I had believed that I had a special relationship with God judging from everything I had experienced in the past.

So I wondered why he was not taking our relationship as seriously as I did even though I've tried to act in ways that would receive his approval.

Yes, it was a decisive moment—the-father-why-have-you-forgotten-me moment. I know God did not create a coward in me, so I summoned the courage and decided to confront him. Then I wondered whether divorcing my wife was such a heinous sin as to deserve the punishing I was getting even though. First, I did not marry in the church; second, she committed adultery and had a baby outside wedlock; worst still, she refused to talk to me about it. So I thought, "How can divorcing such a woman carry so much punishment."

However, I remembered the advice in Matthew 7:7: "Ask and it shall be given you; seek and you shall find." So strengthened by the courage and my faith that my pain was deep enough to earn me God's gracious sympathy, I reached out;

"Almighty God, I am seeking and asking for three things because I do not want to become homeless. First, I want money fast—to make it to another day. Second, a good job. And third, affirm that you are not punished me for divorcing my ex. Losing my family is killing me." Finally, I said, "affirmation in the form of the unusual or miraculous event will be welcome."

Then I stood up in the darkness, trembling. "Almighty God, this is not a prayer. I am asking for a job; I am not begging. I am seeking a good job; I need some money to make it to another day," I lamented.

As in every storm, fear gave way to a fight for survival. So I felt I had not fought hard enough. "He has to hear me. I want answers, and I need to know that he heard me," I thought.

Then I remembered Matthew 6:33: "But seek first the kingdom of God and his righteousness, and all these things shall be added unto you." Then I thought, "Why is it that I keep losing instead of having all these things added unto me?"

Meanwhile, I hit my bed and hurt my wrist; I kicked the bed frame and ripped off my toenail. And I thought, "This can't be happening."

Then the next object I reached was my pillow. So I punched it, I hit it again, and again, and then I punched it repeatedly until feathers began to fly all over the bedroom. Then I felt subdued and said, "Great, two more things have been added to my misery: a broken toenail and a bedroom full of feathers." Then I began to clean the room.

When I finished cleaning my bedroom, I put a bandage on my toe and turned off the light—then I turned it on again and opened my Bible to John 1:12: and read "As many as receive him, to them gave he the right to become the children of God, even to them that believe in his name."

I realized that it had come down to a matter of faith, and reminded God that I named myself Chukudi or Chuks [I believe in God] at the tender age of twelve to profess my solemn and unquestionable faith in him. "I believe in you. I have always been patient and diligent, always trying to do things that will be acceptable to you," I thought. "Grant me that right now at this time of the horrifying disaster, to speak to you. Give me the courage to lift my voice and speak my mind."

I could hardly say another word after that outburst because I did not know what to say next. Then I paused to collect my thoughts. I stood up again, and almost in tears. Then I looked up as if I were looking at God and raised my voice one more time.

"I never intended to divorce Fortune. I endured a lot of pain, I humbled myself before her and before you, and I acted in good faith until my spirit could not take any more abuse," I said. "So forgive me and grant me the affirmation I am seeking. God, if you are not punishing me for the breakdown of that marriage, I ask you to send me that beautiful Jamaican girl I met back when I was in college. Her name is Melba."

I know! To ask God to send a married woman with grown-up children to me was as unrealistic and impractical as it gets. However, I believed in the mystery of his power to do the improbable.

A MATTER OF FAITH

To be honest, I did not intend Melba's visit to be anything physical, romantic, or lustful. It was what came to my mind—something improbable, and specific; something that would make me say, "yes, this is the affirmation I asked for."

I suspected that every pressing demand ought to be accompanied by a pledge to qualify as a valid covenant with God. So in a very subdued voice, I uttered these words: "Father, if you give me a job, I will not miss a day till I retire in 2015. If you give me money, I will not take part in any social event or go to any club. Instead, I will keep to myself until an opportunity that can restore my will to smile and make me happy comes my way. But if you give me a job and send me Melba before 2015, I will quit the job in honor of your grace."

Then I lay down on the floor, and suddenly I fell asleep and began to dream. It was a strange dream—like a movie in which I was the main character from my childhood to that very moment. It was clearly detailed: people I had met, the places I had been, and all my accomplishments and failures. It was the minutest recount of my child and adult lives I had never thought about until that dark moment of my life.

I woke up at five-thirty with a knot in my stomach—hunger pangs I had never experienced until then from not eating the night before. So I lay back in my bed to try to sleep away the pain, but it would not go away.

Then I remembered Data-Com, a company in Flanders, New Jersey. I drove past every day and never bothered to stop and ask for a job. But on that early Saturday morning, I felt I had to go there and ask for a job. Then it dawned on me that I had no means of getting there.

However, my car had been sitting in the parking lot for a year, and I had not even turned it on once, let alone driven it. Now, I needed to go out and check on it mainly to see if I had enough gas in the tank.

Therefore, at five forty-five, I hurried out of my apartment building through the back door to the parking lot.

There was a manhole in the parking lot just outside the back door of the apartment building through which the PSE&G workers went inside to work on the electrical system.

Upon opening the door, I saw a ten-dollar bill on top of that manhole and without wondering how it got there or to whom it belonged. I picked it up, looked up to the sky, and said, "Thank you, God."

And then I walked to my car and found that the tank had gas in it, but the battery was dead, the tires were flat, and the leather seats had cracked—all of them. It was not drivable.

So I called my nephew, Emmanuel, to give me a ride to Data-Com and wait in his car at the parking lot while I dropped off my résumé.

"I will just drop off the résumé. It will take no more than a few minutes," I said. Then I went straight to the HR manager's office, and I knocked on the door.

"Come in," the lady said.

So I walked into the office and gave her my résumé.

"Chuks, did I pronounce it right?" she asked. "Sit down and let me see whether Lou is in yet. He came back from a business trip late last night."

Minutes later, the director, Lou, walked in.

"Hi, my name is Chuks Ndukwe," I greeted.

"You look familiar," he said and glanced over my résumé. "Yes, we met at Lucent Technologies when I was conducting a boot camp there. Let's go and chat in my office," he said.

As we were walking to his office, we talked about the economic crash of 2001 and getting to his office, we chatted some more.

"I have twelve full-time engineers in the field, two full-time engineers in the office Monday through Friday from nine AM to five PM. And two part-time slots: Fridays and Saturdays from five Pm to twelve PM. Another guy works weekends from eleven AM on Saturday to midnight on Sunday. Which of these slots do you want to take?" he asked.

"I would like to work the weekend shift, from eleven on Saturdays to midnight on Sundays," I said.

"Fill out the job application and the W-9 forms, and come to work on Saturday," he said. "The president, Mike, works on weekends. Introduce yourself to him when you see him. I will tell him about the changes. Good luck." Finally, he took me back to Alia's office, shook my hand, and left.

There are moments when, for whatever reason, certain events transcend my understanding. To a large extent, that moment was one of those events.

So amidst filling out of the W-9 and employment application forms, Alia gave me to fill out, the handshaking, and her "Welcome aboard" utterance, I was visibly shaken, almost in tears, and overwhelmed by the fantastic nature of the moment that got me wondering:

> **Why didn't I stop by this company before to ask for a job? If I did could it had turned out the same way it did? Why did I have to be at the verge of homelessness to get the job?**

Finally, why was it that the person who interviewed me was somebody who was familiar with my professional accomplishments and did not need to ask me any question relating to the job?

Regardless, I hurried down the stairs to the parking lot, apologized to Emmanuel for staying too long in the office, and told him "I got the job."

That moment was the pivotal point in my life when the old life gave way for the new and indeed, when my recovery from the most debilitating financial catastrophe I could ever imagine began and continues until today.

Simply put my recovery was nothing short of a miracle or, to put it differently, "A Matter Of Faith."

Chapter 15
Keeping The Pledge

An oath is a frightening thing when you are prepared to keep it, and I felt it tightening around my soul even as I gave my pledge.

~ Rob S. Rice

Now I've had time long enough to absorb the events that took place that night when I went from not having a penny of my own to having ten dollars in a short time—between sunset and sunrise only because I asked for it in the manner I was inspired to pray. Also, I've had time to think about the previous six years nobody cared even to look at my résumé—let alone invite me for interview only to find a job without taking my résumé into consideration—all within a week of asking God to save me.

Without a doubt, the first two of the three things I asked God for; I had received. But the third? I must confess; I had some doubts. After all, what is faith without doubt? Still, my resolve to keep my pledge overshadowed whatever doubt I had.

On that day, I ran down the stairs to the parking lot to tell Emmanuel as he sat in the car—listening to the music that I got the job, I also said, "Take me to Elmwood Park. I want to see whether I can make a deal with Dennis, my mechanic, and get my van back on the road."

When we got to Dennis's shop, I told him that I had found a new job very much like the kind of job I'd been looking for.

"It's about time," he said; Congratulations." Then I said, "Dennis is it OK if I write you a postdated check which you can cash in two weeks when I get paid."

"That won't be a problem Chuks," he said.

A MATTER OF FAITH

Then he released the van to me, and as always, I thanked him again, and then we left the shop.

However, I still needed some money to last me for two weeks, so I called Tunde up and said, "Tunde, I need two hundred dollars, and I'll give you a check which you can cash in two weeks when I get paid."

"OK," he said. "Check or cash?"

"Cash," I said. "I'll be over in thirty minutes."

You might have heard the saying "when it rains, it pours" Well my pouring rain began when I came down with seasonal allergies, which I'd had every spring since I arrived in the United States, just about the only time I get to visit my doctor.

But this time, it was so severe that I was having all kinds of complications. My doctor in Linden, New Jersey, did an EKG, and the test showed that I barely had any electro-cardiac activities on my left side—my left arm, and my left leg.

It was a panic time; my doctor sent me to Trinitas Hospital in Elizabeth, New Jersey for a stress test, and then he did an echo test in his office the following day. I thanked God when the test results came back without revealing any obvious cardiac problem. Still, I was in hell from sleeplessness, whizzing, itching, lung congestion, and difficulty breathing. So my doctor said, "You're arteriosclerotic."

For the above reasons, he recommended an operation immediately to improve the blood circulation throughout my body. He meant to insert a tool through my legs and open the blockage in my arteries. And to that, I said, "I have to think about it. I think I need a second opinion."

"Here's your hospital appointment; I will see you at the Rahway Hospital ER unit," my doctor said.

As it is always the case when it rains and pours, while I was leaving the doctor's office, my phone went off.

"Uncle, your brother has passed on," Ben, my cousin in Ghana told me.

"Ben, what are you saying?" I asked.

"Your brother Dick just passed on," he said. "You've got to come home."

"I can't right now. Do your best and get my brother buried," I said.

"Uncle, tell Emmanuel," he said and hung up.

I could not imagine telling Emmanuel about the death of his father and the prospect of losing his uncle all at the same time. Then a day later, Emmanuel called; I stared at the phone as it rang without me answering it. I was aware that I would stir up angry feelings, but I thought it was better to keep things the way they were than to add additional complications.

"I can explain the situation if I survived the ordeal," I thought. "But if I expired, then everybody would realize that something was seriously wrong—serious enough to prevent me from traveling to Ghana to bury my brother."

✸✸✸

For years, I had listened to Dr. Pressman's radio program on channel 1900 AM, where he talked about a supplement called Nattokinase that he had formulated to break up the hardened protein in the blood to facilitate blood flow throughout the body. I also remembered that during the Nigerian-Biafra War, my legs had been burned by petrochemical fire and I walked over thirty miles running away from gunfire and bomb blasts just minutes after the burn, and I had never received any treatment for my legs.

Moreover, because I had sat in the car for twelve hours every day, delivering parcels, my legs had begun to harden, itch, cramp, and burn. Until that moment, the EKG showed that blood was barely flowing throughout my body.

Although the thought of dying did not cross my mind, I was keenly aware that I had begun to dry up for each time I stood in front of the mirror, I'd see cobweb of wrinkles on my face and feel the hardened parts of my thighs and legs.

To some extent, though, my will to not look too wrinkly in death rather than the will to live compelled me to take unusual steps to deal with the situation. So I called Dr. Pressman's office and ordered a few bottles of the supplement.

A few weeks later, I received the supplement—nattokinase and began to take it. Shortly my legs, thighs, and butt started to hemorrhage, proving that the supplement was breaking down the hardened protein in my blood into soluble particles and forcing them to exit my body through the skin.

Still, I did not miss a day of work—a part of the pledge I made to God. I wrapped my legs with bandages and wore layers of pants to prevent blood from showing. Also, I changed my bedding sheets from white to black to hide the bloodstains and did laundry every day.

For a while, the hardened parts of my legs and thighs did not show any sign of softening. This was not surprising, because I was still sitting down for over twelve hours in my van, delivering parcels.

Dumb, stupid, or merely scared, I bought a set of files and began to file down those hardened spots on my thighs and legs. And I just let the damaged spots heal. The feeling was excruciating most of the time as if I had pieces of pins sticking out of my skin; taking a bath was very challenging due to the biting feeling from soap and water. The worst part was drying my body. Still, I persevere.

Shortly, the bleeding spread to my hands, back, and face, and there were a few spots on my head too. This ordeal lasted for two years before my body began to heal and grow new skin cells; the wrinkles caused by the hardening skin started to go away gradually.

Far from my mind at that time was the affirmation I had asked God for—to send Melba to lift my spirit up.

But unexpectedly, I was at work one day in June 2012; I had just finished solving a complicated network problem that took about one hour. Then my phone went off.

"Hello, this is Chuks," I answered.

"It's me, Delsey, Melba's sister," the caller said.

"What a surprise!" I screamed.

"Yes, it's been a long time, hasn't it?"

"My God, Delsey, I thought I had lost you forever," I said.

"Don't be silly. You are always on my mind. I will never forget you," Delsey said. "Somebody wants your number."

"Who wants my number?" I asked.

"Oh my God, don't tell me you've forgotten my sister Melba," she said.

"How are she, her husband, and children?" I inquired.

"Her children have all graduated from college, and she is practicing law in Michigan," she said. "Can I give her your number?"

"Yes, by all means, do," I said.

"Chuks, I'm just passing your first house on Wilmington Street," she said. "I live in Brockton now, not too far from that house. I will give Melba your number. Call me sometimes."

"OK, Delsey, I will," I said.

"OK, bye, Chuks. It was nice talking to you," she said and hung up.

Then two months later, on Sunday night, I called Melba from work. We talked for two hours, reminiscing over the past. Then she said, "Chuks, I am coming to see you, but you must send me a ticket."

"OK, but you have to wait till 2015," I said.

Probably you are wondering, "why didn't he jump up for joy when Melba told him that she was coming to see him? The answer is simple "I was not in any condition to see Melba yet. I wished she could wait until I recovered a little. Simply put, I looked too ugly to see her." Then she said, "Look, my friend, if you force me to buy my ticket, I will not be happy about it." So I gave in and said, "OK, stay on the line." Then I called Expedia while she waited, and we made her reservation for August 10, 2012, and I let her take comfort in knowing that the visit was her idea, and I did not resist.

On August 10, I was dropping off auto parts at Towne Auto Collision, in Randolph, New Jersey, when my phone went off.

"Hello, this is Melba. I am at the airport. My plane will be arriving at Newark Airport at eleven forty-five," she said.

"All right, I will be waiting at the arrival gate," I responded.

Her visit—the affirmation I asked God for became a reality when she arrived at the airport at 11:50 p.m. I was standing outside the gate as she approached the waiting area watching every step Melba took, waving my hands in the air to make sure she saw me. I was afraid she would not recognize me after everything I had gone through, and the natural damage ageing inflicts on people.

At last, we hugged and went down to the baggage carousel area and waited for her luggage.

"Here comes my bag. I didn't bring much, because I didn't know how much time you'd have for me," Melba said.

Feeling as though happy days were upon us again, we spent five days together, going to Atlantic City, walking around the beach, and then playing slot machines at different casinos, and did some shopping too.

On Monday—Melba's last day with me, I went to work and came home before she woke up at eleven forty-five in the morning to be exact; she did not even know that I had been to work and back. Then after lunch, I escorted her to the airport.

And there at the check-in area, we chatted for a while before we strolled to the boarding gate. Finally, we hugged, and I watched Melba turn and walk away until she vanished behind the boarding gate.

When I returned home, I realized that at least a tiny portion of the Bible has proven right for me since I've asked and I received what I asked for. Still, I had to keep every one of my pledges.

Three months after Melba's visit, I quit my job at Data-Com on December 30, 2012, to fulfil that part of my pledge.

Meanwhile, my health had begun to improve as the good O' oxygen-rich blood had started to find its way through my veins, judging from the increase in my pulse rate.

However, I still kept to myself waiting for something unique to drag me out of this keeping-to-myself pledge, which at the time did not seem likely.

One day, I ran into my nephew, Emmanuel. We had not spoken or met since his father passed. I had tried to avoid talking to him until I was ready to discuss everything that had been happening to me.

"Hi, Uncle," he greeted me.

"Emma, how are you?" I asked.

He was on the phone, talking to his girlfriend, and surprisingly, he did not seem angry.

"Say hi to Pamala," he said.

"Hello, my name is Chuks; Emmanuel's uncle," I said.

"My name is Pamala. It is nice talking to you," his girlfriend said.

"It's nice talking to you too, Pam," I said.

Chuks I, Ndukwe

At first, it did not seem evident that our meeting would lead to that momentous event I had asked God for—to fulfil my final pledge of staying to myself until late in spring of 2013 when I received a wedding invitation from Emmanuel. I was glad to hear that he was getting married to Pamala on August 17, 2013. Then I remembered my pledge.

"Good Lord, thank you, Almighty Father," I thought. "That's an opportunity for me to break out of the *I will keeping-to-myself pledge*."

I had not met Pamala before, so I quickly logged into the website they had set up for their wedding announcement. After reading the piece, they wrote about themselves and their proposal and looking at her picture, I did not need anybody to tell me anything about her. She looked beautiful, and she wrote brilliantly. Still, I wanted to meet her before the wedding—a proper thing to do if you are the groom's uncle.

One week before the wedding, my nephew, Chima, called me up.

"Uncle, can you join us on Friday?" he asked. "We are having a welcome party for Pamala and her family."

"Definitely, I will be there," I replied.

In the evening of the party, Chima met me at the door when I arrived—one hour earlier than other guests. I was in a happy mood, excited to be free to attend the party and to see that girl walk through the door. I joked around with the kids, CJ, Chisom, and Ugo Jr. The kids were happy to see me, and I was thrilled to be with them, too, after five years of staying to myself.

"Oh my God, Uncle Chuks, where have you been hiding? It's been a long time since I saw you last," Ugo Jr. said.

"I've been having issues with my father and waiting for him to answer a few questions," I replied.

"What are you talking about, Uncle? Isn't your father dead?" she asked. Then I replied, "I don't mean that father. I am talking about my heavenly father." And then she said, "I am thrilled to see you, Uncle Chuks."

"It's good to see you all," I replied.

"Uncle, how are you?" Chima greeted.

"Better than ever now that I am here with all of you," I said.

I had bought a bottle of champagne for the bride and groom's toast. So I gave it to Chima to save for the occasion.

A MATTER OF FAITH

At five o'clock, guests began to stroll in, and then one hour later, the house was full of people.

Suddenly, the doorbell sounded. Nenna Chima, my nephew's wife, opened the door, and a group of people strolled in, followed by Emmanuel. Then a young lady walked in behind him.

"Uncle, this is Pamala and Pam, this is Uncle Chuks," Chima introduced us.

"Hi, Pam, I am glad to meet you," I responded finally.

"I am glad to meet you, Uncle Chuks," Pam replied.

Chima went around the room and introduced me to Pamala's family members. And then he turned to one couple and said, "Uncle, meet Reverend, and Mrs. Gardiner, Pam's parents. Reverend and Mrs. Gardiner, this is our uncle, Chuks."

"I am delighted to meet you, Reverend and Mrs. Gardiner," I said.

"The pleasure is ours," Reverend Gardiner replied.

Then Chima continued to introduce me to Pam's sisters, nieces, and cousins. That was my first time appearing at a social gathering in five years, so I was rusty in the beginning, but as time went on, I began to relax.

A few minutes later, Tunde, walked in with his wife, my niece Mr. Grace Adewunmi.

"Oh my God, Uncle Chuks is here!" My niece screamed.

"Yes, my dear, I am here, by God's grace, and I am thrilled to see you. How are you, Tunde?" I greeted them.

"One day at a time, Uncle. How are you?" Tunde inquired; then we embraced.

As the party got underway, I walked to the dining room to get a soft drink and got hit by the inviting aroma of irresistible, delicious and mouthwatering food—arranged in a ready-to-be served fashion.

Obviously, because of what the event meant to me, I'd be remiss if I failed to admit my state of euphoric exuberance. At dinner, I sat with Reverend Gardiner and chatted about our families, Nigeria, Turks and Caicos, and life in America.

Halfway through the reception, Tunde stood up with a bottle of champagne in his hand. Got everybody's attention, and said, "I wish to call on Uncle Chuks to toast the bride and the bridegroom. Uncle"

I did not expect the honor; all I was longing for was to meet Pamala before the wedding. However, I managed to say a few words to wish the young couple happiness in their lives together, and I reassured the bride's family that their daughter was safe as a member of our family.

The wedding took place the following day at the Renaissance Hotel in Woodbridge, New Jersey. So I drove to Woodbridge with my girlfriend Crissy, we checked in and relaxed a little before the guests began to arrive.

Then at four o'clock, I got dressed and went down to the lobby to check out the atmosphere and found Reverend Gardiner chatting with Tunde. So we chatted for a while before I went upstairs to get Crissy.

The ceremony was short and beautiful, and then we hung around for an hour while the photographer took pictures, and the guests and their families greeted each other and shared conversations.

When we returned to the reception area, guests gave their names to ushers who directed them to their seats. But looking through the list, I discovered that my name was not on the list, so I approached one of the ushers and informed him. Surprisingly instead of helping, he pushed me aside and told me that my name was not on the list because I was not invited.

"Sir, the groom is my nephew," I said. "How could I not be invited?"

"This event is not about you sir, OK?" the usher said, sounding really nasty and disrespectful.

"Is it possible that at least one sheet of the list is missing?" I inquired. Then the usher shouted, "Move out of the way, and let the invited guests get in."

As he was pushing me aside the second time, a voice called out to me from inside the hall and said, "Uncle, come on in." Therefore, I turned and saw the bride's cousin waving Crissy and me in then I realized the voice was his. So we followed him to a table where other family members flanked Crissy and me on both sides. Then a few minutes later, the waiter passed out the menus.

A MATTER OF FAITH

"Chuks, they have two things you don't like, steak, and chicken, on the menu. What would you like?" Crissy asked.

"Chicken will be fine," I said.

The food was delicious too. While servers cleared the dining tables, I chatted with the bride's parents and asked Reverend and Mrs. Gardiner, "What would you like to drink?"

"Just what we are drinking, we don't drink liquor," Reverend Gardiner said.

"That makes three of us," I replied. Then Reverend Gardiner added, "Loud music bothers my ears, so we will just return to our room. Have fun."

After the bride and the groom's toasts, the music played all night, and so I danced all night with every member of the bride's family, male, and female. At some point, I went back to my hotel room and changed my clothes because I was sweaty from dancing.

I had so much fun and wished the party would never end, but at some point past midnight, the lights went dim, and the hotel workers began to break down the set. Then I sat on the floor with the bride's relatives and discussed the event—joking and laughing.

"When will you come to Turk's and Caicos for a visit?" they asked.

"After retiring in 2015," I said.

We enjoyed each other so much that we sat on that floor and chatted until the security guards threw us out of the hall. Obviously, it was as if we had known each other forever.

"Uncle Chuks, we were nervous about this marriage," the bride's sister said. "But after your toast last night, we felt good, happy, and reassured that Pam is joining a wonderful family like yours."

"Thank you, that's very kind of you," I replied. "What's the plan for tomorrow?"

"I am my father's baby, so I am going back on Monday with my parents, but everybody else is going back tomorrow," the bride's youngest brother said.

"Are they departing from Newark?" I inquired.

"No, they are flying from JFK," the boy said.

"Who is taking them to New York?" I asked.

"We don't know yet," he said. Then I told them, "I'll see you tomorrow morning to make sure they have transportation to New York." And then I went upstairs to my room.

After breakfast—the following morning, I called the taxi office and requested for a service, so when the cab driver arrived, I prepaid him to take the bride's siblings to JFK.

Simply stated, Emmanuel's wedding was the opportunity I asked God to end my "I will keep-to-myself pledge." Without a doubt, God had granted everything I asked for, and I also kept my pledge. And now I was back to the flow of normal living—what a fantastic experience.

Similarly, making pledges the way I did and keeping every promise as God granted each of what I asked for and allowed my spirit to bask in the glory of the covenant by which he granted redemption and salvation to humanity through the suffering and death of Jesus Christ.

Here's how my normal life which I had kept to myself resumed; Emmanuel visited me the following Saturday, the first visit since his father passed. So I congratulated him one more time and extended my condolences for the death of his father—my only brother whose well being and business success I had had on my mind forever.

For the most part, that's how I hoped Emmanuel would learn about what I went through. So we chatted for a while, and then he called his mother in Ghana. In the same way, I did Emmanuel, we had not talked since her husband died. However, without telling her my reasons for not coming home to bury her husband, we had a normal conversation—the kind typical of a functioning family.

"Uncle, do you go to church?" she asked.

"No, I stopped going to church," I said. "I can't stand the hypocrisy of the so-called churchgoers. But believe me, I'm a Christian and in good standing with God."

"I want you to start going to church," she persuaded me.

"OK, my dear," I replied.

"When are we going to see you again?" she asked.

"I will visit as soon as I retire. I would not like to think about work when I come to visit," I said.

"When will that be?" she asked.

"Hopefully by the end of 2015," I said.

A MATTER OF FAITH

"Uncle, I am glad to hear from you," she said. "I would like you and Emma to start talking to each other again."

"We will, my dear."

"I want you two to stay close. You are all I've got now."

"His marriage has changed everything."

"Uncle, I want to be hearing from you," she said. "Bye."

"OK, my dear, Bye," I replied.

At that moment, I realized that everything had changed for good. Therefore, I upgraded my phone plan to be able to communicate with my family members in Ghana more often.

One day, I got a call from my nephew, Chima.

"Uncle, I had a conversation with Dr. Kanu Maduka," he said. "He wants you to call him."

So a few weeks later, I called Dr. Maduka.

"Uncle, it's me, Chuks I. Ndukwe," I said.

"Ogbuleke, how are you?" he inquired, calling me by my birth name.

"Chima told me that you had asked about me. How are you?"

"Yes, he told me that you are back on your feet."

"That's true Uncle, God has been good to me."

"Ogbuleke, there was no doubt in my mind that you would bounce back," he said. "Right from your childhood to this moment, your life has been a miracle."

"Thank you."

"I mean it. You've exemplified yourself in everything you've done. I hope you'd find time to reach out to our young people and teach them how to be successful."

Although I appreciated his compliments, still I questioned the integrity of what he said about me being successful after the catastrophic failure I was recovering from.

In conclusion, when I step back and think about my shortcomings, my limitations, my achievements, failures, and survival, I can't help but marvel at the audacity with which my inner-power ploughed through every obstacle I faced.

For the most part, it's the oscillation between inspiration and tragedy, and ultimately, my miraculous recovery from the verge of homelessness that inspired me to write this memoir, "A Matter Of faith."

Epilogue

The only true wisdom is in knowing you know nothing.

~ Socrates

Seventeen years had gone by since my professional career ended. Twelve years since I began driving around from New Jersey to Baltimore, Maryland, and beyond delivering parcels, pharmaceutical products, and auto parts. It is a different world now from the one before, the one I used to live in—a familiar world. I have met and learned a lot from people of all ages, of different nationalities and walks of life.

The truth is that I have gotten smarter—I mean street smarter. I can talk to people and have a sense of where they are coming from and empathize with them. I can speak to a homeless person and share not only his pain but a few dollars out of the ten I set aside to share with the homeless—each month when I get my social security check. It is the least I could do to memorialize that ten-dollar bill God gave me to jump-start my life. That morning my previous experience came crashing down, and I was a couple of hours away from knocking at the doors of the homeless shelter to ask for a bed.

I have learned that when you are trying to solve a problem, others reach out and grab at you. And when you are trying to put your broken life back together, issues paw and gnaw at you.

I even had an experience once when amidst chaos, fear, and uncertainty about my future, a drunken man, maybe a drug addict, tried to give me advice on how to deal with my problems. I must admit he burned me by doing that.

However, now I realize I was wrong to be mad at him. Because he saw life through his kaleidoscope—the prism in his mind, through which he sees everything—in fact, he meant well.

By any objective measures, my life has been nothing but active, although chaotic sometimes—a fair price to pay for immunity against boredom. There has not been a dull moment, or time wasted worrying about what people did or did not do to me.

Now, my problem is minor. I am old and retired, and many things have lost their vigor and magic. It is not that I do not care anymore. It's the way things are. Ordinary things—the ones we adore, they lose their novelty and charm. And the new ones—the ones young people are passionate about—well, I confess to unintentional snobbery; they fail to meet the rigor and artistry of the ones gone by. Still, I let young people take comfort in knowing that they will do better than my generation. It is the way it has always been.

When I finished the final draft of this manuscript, I let a few neighbors read it for comments, and as you would expect, some offered valuable hard-to-ignore comments and suggestions.

So while correcting the errors I found in the manuscript, I kept thinking about the day I chose Chukudi or Chuks [I believe in God] for my baptismal name to profess my solemn belief and faith in God. And wondered how I could have known that one day that declaring would eventually become an impelling force—a stone upon which I planted my feet when I asked God for rescue the way I did—the day I lost everything I owned to the last penny.

I want the reader to know that losing a job and not finding another for years is normal, especially at times, such as the economic recession. And losing everything for a good cause is not unheard of either.

But on the flip side, to ask God to rescue me the way I did and expected a result instantly was insane. To ask God to send my ex-girlfriend, who was married with adult children to visit me, was unreasonable. Believing that she would lift my spirit and affirm the righteousness of my divorce, was wishful; I admit to its transcending of the false devotion, instinctive courtesy, and mere good manners while praying.

For the most part, though, asking God for rescue and making pledges the way I did remind me of the covenant by which God granted redemption and salvation to humanity through the suffering and death of Jesus Christ.

On the periphery, some may think that the way I asked God for rescue was an act of rudeness. I know because a young girl, Ebony who

A MATTER OF FAITH

had read the manuscript came to my apartment with her grandmother and said, "You acted nasty to God in your book, and you need to apologize for acting that way."

"Please have a seat," I said to her and her grandmother and offered them some Tostitos chips and Cranberry juice. Then I thanked her and her grandmother for reading the manuscript, and for her thoughtfulness. Then I asked her, "Do you remember what Jesus did when he was overcome by pain and suffering while he was nailed to the cross?"

"Yeah! Everybody knows that" she said. "Father, Father, why have you forsaken me." Then I continued, "OK, what if you are in serious pain, and there is nobody around to help you; what will you do?"

"I will send for my grandma."

"What if Grandma could not be reached?"

"I will cry," she said.

"Well my dear, what you read in that book was not only my cry for rescue," I said "it was also my father-father-why-have-you-forsaken-me moment. Aren't you amazed by how fast God heard my cry and came to my rescue?" I asked her.

"I can't believe it," she said, "Grandma said that you are smart, and she is right." She closed the book.

Finally, I told Ebony that although it is not apparent for lack of awareness and spiritual rigor, we all have a relationship with God. For me, when kneeling down, clasping hands, closing eyes, and praying with faked timidity fail to produce the result I want, I've no problem doing what a reasonable person in a relationship would do. —Remind the person you're in a relationship with why your request deserves serious consideration and make a deal if necessary. Ebony's strong reaction to how I asked God for rescue in this book helped me to clarify some blurry and not-well-articulated thoughts.

Sure, there are moments when I lay back and think about that metaphoric journey—life. I marvel at its twists and turns, ups and downs, trials and tribulations. And then I realize that there's not a single thing I have done in my life that happened out of my genius or brilliant ideas—in fact, most of my well-thought-out plans don't work out well or as planned—honestly, they always end up in smoke.

So I realized that inside each one of us is an interiority complex—the inner-power, the guide; conscience, the arbiter between good and evil; non-carnal senses that sees past the bright light of the day and the darkness of night to preview the events that are yet to unfold; the inner-voice that counsels the physical self. And these four elements of life function in contingent symbiosis to take care of our worries and move the journey along—within the guardrails of the natural order.

If this perspective on the journey of life were not real. How then could I have made it to this point in time?

In *The Courage To Aspire*, I wrote about the old lady I helped cross the railroad track in the town of Umuahia in Abia state, Nigeria who vanished after our short meeting—Yes, I can see and hear her saying, "Your life in the US will be difficult, but the end will be just fine."

I must admit, the first part of her pronouncements have come to pass. But as for the end? I am not quite sure of what she meant.

However, now I wake up every morning not worrying about anything, and I wish every living soul could enjoy a worry-free life such as I feel today.

Most importantly, I do not owe anybody, hate, or hold any ill feelings towards anybody.

Simply stated, when I lay down or sit in front of my computer to write, I can feel the gentle flow of fresh air permeating every part of my vein. In contrast to when I was drying up from the effects of the world I left behind, and then I wonder if that is what the old lady meant by "the end will be just fine." But for me, it's all *A Matter Of Faith*.

Acknowledgements

I have to begin with a stranger, Dr. Ekpo Ekong. We met on the plane the day I was leaving Nigeria for the United States. When he realized that I did not know anything about the country of my destination, he adopted me instantly. And supported me throughout the early days of my life in the United States.

I want to express my gratitude to the lady I lived with when I first arrived in the United States, Mrs. Terry Zdanauk. She made me feel welcome and comfortable in the town of Burlington, Massachusetts, where I was the only black man around. My assimilation into her family gave me a unique and broader perspective as to how uplifting the nondiscriminatory environment can be. Moreover, she was extremely patient with my ignorance and naiveté of American culture and ways of life and helped me to catch on.

Miss Wendy lived across the street from Terry. From her porch, she watched the dogs chase after me back and forth on my way to and from school, and work, and she gave me a brand-new Toyota Corolla to keep the dogs away from me. So I owe her a world of gratitude.

I want to thank my realtor, Mr. Schumer. Even before the thought of buying a house came to my mind, he persuaded me to buy one. He gave me his own money to make down payment on the house he sold to me as a reward for my act of goodness towards him. So I thank him for that.

Of course, I thank the total stranger. He heard the story of my financial demise, and he gave me a van, a Ford E250. Their acts of kindness brought the phrase "American generosity" home to me. For that, I am grateful.

Finally, I want to thank my niece Grace; her husband, Tunde; my nephew Chima; and his wife, Nenna, for their support when I was going through the worst part of my living experiences.

Chuks I, Ndukwe

    I hope that my unconditional love for them makes up, in a little way, for my failure to live up to their expectations as the elder of our extended families.
    I want to express my sincere appreciation to my editors, Devon and Anton for the job they did in shaping this narrative.

About the Author

Chuks I. Ndukwe was once a sought after engineer in the High Tech industry. He graduated from Northeastern University in Boston, Massachusetts and worked for such companies as Codex Corporation, USRobotics, ADC Telecom, and Lucent Technologies where he mentored junior engineers and managed research and development departments.

During his career, Ndukwe demonstrated strategic management skills, and his problem-solving skills earned him "Key Contributor Award" at ADC Telecom, Minnetonka Minnesota. He built a strong team of engineers that performed above expectations—designing such technologies as caller identification, modems, routers, and Internet gateways.

Ndukwe is now retired and lives in Newark, New Jersey where he devotes his time writing to inspire others.

Other Books By Chuks I. Ndukwe

Like this Book?

If you enjoyed this book, below is another book
by **Chuks I. Ndukwe**

The Courage To Aspire
(Trade Paperback)

Distributed by Ingram and Available on Amazon, ikebiebooks.com,
and everywhere books are sold

www.ingramcontent.com/pod-product-compliance
Lightning Source LLC
Chambersburg PA
CBHW070736020526
44118CB00035B/1370